HÉLÈNE BARNEKOW

with Nina Pettersson

POWER with MEANING

Values-based leadership in a changing world

authorHOUSE®

AuthorHouse™ UK
1663 Liberty Drive
Bloomington, IN 47403 USA
www.authorhouse.co.uk
Phone: UK TFN: 0800 0148641 (Toll Free inside the UK)
        UK Local: (02) 0369 56322 (+44 20 3695 6322 from outside the UK)

Published by AuthorHouse   02/05/2024

ISBN: 979-8-8230-8622-6 (sc)
ISBN: 979-8-8230-8623-3 (e)

Library of Congress Control Number: 2024901879

Print information available on the last page.

This book is printed on acid-free paper.

Graphic Design: Tadhg Amin

Contents

Preface – ix

Preface to the English edition – xi

Introduction: A way forward – xiii

1

It will soon pass – 1

A paradigm shift – 4
Four key conditions – 5
Customer obsession – 7

2

Why am I here? – 17

Something to lean on – 18
Trust in common sense – 21
Walk the talk – 22
My true north — and ours – 24
Want to join the journey? – 27
Employee obsession – 28

3

No more people like you – 37

Moving out there — static in here – 38
Diversity out there — uniformity in here – 41
Life under the microscope – 45
Birds of a feather – 46
But we rode a Segway together! – 48

(4)

Ear to the ground – 53

On the customer's terms – 53
When everything and everyone communicates – 54
Communication for innovation – 55
The ideas that come from outside – 56
The ideas that come from within – 58
Communicative leadership – 61

(5)

The power of storytelling – 67

The house is on fire! – 68
Pride as a springboard – 69
Storydoing — bringing the story to life – 71
Talk the walk – 72
The never-ending story – 73

(6)

The fearless organization – 79

Belts and suspenders – 80
Self-esteem and self-confidence – 81
Fearless leadership – 87
Lines a little too straight? – 89

(7)

Super magnets – 95

The age of transparency – 96
The gratifying gap – 97
Inside and out – 100
For a hundred years or more – 101

Conclusion: No turning back – 105

Thank you – 107

About the author– 107

References – 109

Preface

Leading change in this day and age is like running a marathon with the power and mentality of a sprinter. Not only do changes often have to happen quickly, but they can be more profound and require more of the whole organization than anyone could have imagined. We may discover that old structures that we have built up over a long time are standing in our way. Or we realize that the entire organizational culture — how we think and how we organize our work — makes us slower or more cautious than we need to be. To survive, we may need to reinvent ourselves in some way. We may need a reboot. I believe we are at a crossroads where we need to dare to question old ways of managing and organizing and explore something new, something that we have not yet fully grasped. A long-term — and more radical — change, which affects everyone in an organization, is not a project. It does not happen overnight because it requires 50, 5,000 or even 50,000 employees to be willing, able, and daring to drive the change forward, every day. Otherwise, the ball will soon roll back again. This book is based on my experience leading change in various roles at large international companies. It's the result of many long conversations with writer and editor Nina Pettersson. Nina and I have talked about issues that are close to my heart:

> collaboration, diversity and inclusion, courage, trust, self leadership, communication, responsiveness, and — not least of all — values-based leadership. I have shared my lessons from a long professional life and also tried to put into words what I believe in and am passionate about. Nina has listened and asked questions and written. During our discussions, the outline of what I would call a "platform for change" became increasingly clear. Each chapter of the book describes an aspect of that platform and seeks to answer the question: *How can you create the energy and drive needed to bring about real change?*

I see a future beyond micromanagement, silo structures, and silo mentality, one where we collaborate more across borders, are more responsive to the outside world and to each other, and see more trust and less control. I see an everyday life at work where more people can be themselves, more people can be creative, more people can learn, and more people can feel passionate about what they do. We have come some of the way, but we are far from there. To succeed, I think we all — especially those of us who have been entrusted to lead others — need to stop and ask ourselves what we believe in and stand for deep down. For the answer that we need to lean on and draw strength from during this journey.

Hélène Barnekow Stockholm, May 22, 2019

Preface to the English edition

Ever since I launched my book Restart in Swedish, I must have answered hundreds of messages asking when it would be made available in English. Given my background with the privilege of having lived and worked in so many countries, I always wanted to share these reflections with my non-Swedish-speaking community, but it always felt like too big a project, and there was never enough time.

But as technology improved and software engineer Tadhg Amin came into my life – the text could be translated by DeepL, improved by GPT, and then proofread by both of us – I suddenly had a decent enough translation that could be handed over to my friends at Svengard & Co. to review and proofread. Seeing my book finally come alive in English is really another milestone moment on my quest to drive conversation around what I believe is one of society's most important questions: how do we help leaders think more broadly about their leadership platforms than delivering on a number of quarterly KPIs? What do leaders – and team members – need to be able to make their organizations thrive in these fast-moving times as we keep our teams feeling good about what they do and how they do it?

The background to Re:start is my professional life as a leader across several international companies and across many countries and continents: Ericsson, Sony Ericsson, EMC (now Dell EMC), and then returning to Sweden to join the Swedish telecoms operator Telia. When this book was originally published, I joined Microsoft as CEO of their Swedish operations. I could have easily added insights and experiences from that position that fit right into this book.

As I reread the material, I kept the mindset of asking myself whether it was still relevant. And at least I think so, and I hope readers do as well. In essence, I think we talk too much about change leadership and change management. I think we need to focus on building organizations with values-based leadership geared towards managing and leading in an ever-changing world. This is our biggest challenge as leaders – and our greatest opportunity. Every chapter reflects the lessons I've learned about what you need to address to get those valuesbased fundamentals in place – all while you build up your teams and your organization to both deliver on customer expectations and the teams' expectations. Ultimately, I believe that organizations urgently need to become super magnets – places where customers really want to be customers, talent wants to work, partners want to partner, and investors want to invest. If that's our ultimate goal, and we succeed, then we can be sure that our financial returns will follow and we'll be able to manage through good times and bad while still holding on to our vision and purpose, even when the road ahead will require a few adjustments.

As I worked with the book in English, it also became increasingly clear from the feedback that the original name that I wanted for the book became more relevant than ever: *Power with Meaning*. Every leadership role means power in some sort or shape. Every leader has a choice to make if that power platform is used with purpose or not. The world needs infinitely more leaders using their power with meaning – so renaming the book from *Re.start* to *Power with Meaning* became a natural next step.

Leadership roles in 2023 are not for the faint of heart. They take courage – a lot of courage – to manage the complex stakeholder map, the fast-changing times, the demanding customers, the employees, and the constant influx of new technology. And it takes humility to realize that we don't know everything, that we truly need diverse perspectives in the room and need to be curious about what we don't know. I'm hoping the book will continue to spark dialogue and get more leaders and teams into doing in the directions that we set as our own. Because that's what leadership is, more than anything else: setting the tone from the top, of course, but then focusing on what you actually do every day as a leader to walk that talk and be that movement forward.

Thank you to Nina Pettersson, with whom I had the opportunity to create this book in Swedish. Without you, this work would never have existed. Thank you to all my teams, colleagues, and leaders, and to the many communities I have been a part of across the world. You challenged me, encouraged me, supported me, and brought me back to earth when I took off too far and too fast. And not the least, thank you for letting me experiment with leadership. That gave me the opportunity to use my leadership platform for impact far outside the normal quarterly focus – and for that, I am forever grateful.

Hélène Barnekow
Stockholm October 15 2023

Introduction:
A way forward

Artificial intelligence, big data, and block-chain solutions, automation and robotics, 3D printing, the Internet of Things, virtual and augmented realities, and much more. The future is being hammered out in lines of code, and it's happening fast. Then, add globalization and demographic changes, new sustainability requirements, new values, new lifestyles, and other megatrends. And perhaps most importantly, climate change.

This tidal wave is hitting us all with full force. Every market and organization is affected, every society, every part of the world. Old structures, values, and behaviors are questioned. What was once successful suddenly turns out to be ineffective. Previously profitable business models and strategies are abandoned, and even giants fall. The list of established companies that have struggled to innovate and change is long, including Kodak and Nokia Mobile Phones two of the most famous. And yet, if we think the pace of change is fast now, we should take a deep breath and accept that it will never be this slow again.

Not so long ago, many companies were able to form a relatively clear picture of the immediate future. Targets were set, and the budget provided guidance throughout the year. The conditions were more or less a given, and the hierarchy of responsibilities was clear. The plan was made, the map drawn. Then, you stepped forward. One group of specialists completed their part of the work and passed the baton to the next group of specialists, often in closed rooms. The customer was rarely invited or allowed to have any real impact. However, the documentation — for example, in the form of instructions and requirement specifications — was often impressive in its scope. This was one of several reasons why the processes could and did take time. There wasn't much room to make any missteps in the terrain or to rethink anything at all in the middle of an ongoing process.

Now it's different.

Someone described it as standing with a heavy backpack by a rapids, perhaps a roaring alpine stream up in Sarek National Park. If the water level was previously low and many rocks stuck up above the surface, the water is now high and flowing. Before, you could stand there at the water's edge and plan: "I'm going to get from here to *there*. First, I'll take that stone, then this one, then that one. Then I'll finally get across and end up right on the path that leads on." Now the beach on the other side is shrouded in fog. It's unclear how wide the rapids are or which direction to take. The water hides the contours of the rocks. There is a high risk of slipping and being swept away by the current. The force of the water causes sand and gravel, even stones, to move under the surface.

On top of that, you're in a hurry.

Most companies have long since realized that it is not possible to just do nothing, in the sense of "doing what you have always done." Change is the new normal. Nobody wants to be slow, but adaptable, agile, and innovative, maybe even disruptive.

But how do you do it?

This book is based on nearly 40 hours of intensive conversations with Hélène Barnekow, one of Sweden's most celebrated female business leaders. She has more than 25 years of experience in the IT, mobile, and telecom industry, a long international career, and, at the time of writing, has just taken over as CEO of Microsoft Sweden.

In the spring of 2015, Hélène assumed the role of CEO of Telia Sweden and, for a few years, led the company through a revolutionary change process. The journey was part reorganization, part digital transformation, and part cultural change. At Telia, Hélène talked a lot about the importance of putting the customer at the center. "Customer obsession" became one of the brightest guiding lights during the change process. In fact, during her years at Telia, she spoke so often and so much about customer obsession that it would have been perfectly reasonable to make it the title of the book.

But anyone who spends a moment with Hélène realizes that customer obsession is just one piece of a much larger puzzle. If the overall goal is to better equip the organization for the future, customer obsession is not the only means but one of several. Building strong teams is another. And if Hélène personifies the idea of customer obsession, she equally personifies courageous, present, and human leadership. She has made a name for herself by empowering and uplifting people in a way that contributes to change. In everything Hélène does and stands for, everything we explore in more detail in the seven chapters of the book, customer obsession isn't really the common element. Rather, at the core is the desire to set something in motion, to drive — even *push* — change.

This book revolves around Hélène's thoughts on and experiences of leading change, but Hélène has not held the pen herself. She has sat in the interview chair. The book also borrows many ideas from researchers, authors, and others who have already thought about the issues we discuss here. Their conclusions highlight and reinforce in various ways what Hélène herself finds natural and obvious. The book is also based on interviews with some of the people, including former colleagues, who have been closest to Hélène throughout her professional life, especially in recent years. Their perspectives on Hélène's leadership and their many examples of what she has done in practice have been invaluable.

This book is about creating a movement towards a more adaptive, communicative, and innovative organizational culture. Not in a small young start-up company, but in an established organization with thousands of employees. It's also about the importance of leadership in our time. The book is aimed at leaders at all levels who see the need for a more profound change internally, as well as anyone interested in the organizations and leadership of the future. It is not a manual, does not present a method, has no step-by-step "do this and you will succeed." After all, conditions are different for every organization and every time. Moreover, the kind of change we are talking about here has no beginning and no end. You don't finish. But the book describes a platform, a philosophy, or an approach and shows different ways to act on that platform.

The first chapter — *It will soon pass* — deals with the difference between a project that has a clear starting point and finish line and a profound long-term change to an entire organizational culture.

Here, we also address customer obsession as one of the most powerful drivers of that process.

The second chapter — *Why am I here?* — focuses on the very foundation of the change journey: the answer to the question why. Why are we doing this? And why am I here, right now? Here, we also consider the customer obsession's closest ally: the employee obsession.

The third chapter — *No more people like you* — is about diversity and inclusion and the importance of real cooperation: within the team, within the organization, and with the outside world.

The fourth chapter — *Ear to the ground* — describes the characteristics of a communicative organization and communicative leadership. Here, we highlight responsiveness as a cornerstone of an innovative culture.

The fifth chapter — *The power of storytelling* — focuses on storytelling and storydoing, showing in words and actions what the journey is all about.

The sixth chapter — *The fearless organization* — illustrates that it is not enough to be willing and able to change: we must also dare. This is about how we can create a culture where we dare to question, dare to rethink and innovate, and dare to be fully ourselves.

The seventh chapter — *The super magnet* — discusses what it takes to stay attractive as an employer today and in the future.

Hélène herself is not a big fan of "pre-meetings," so let's not dwell on the contents of the book, but simply dive in.

I t is August 2011. Just a few years later, the message "digitalization changes everything" will be repeated endlessly, and it will have become a universal truth.

But we are not quite there yet. This late summer, Belgian Philippe Gosseye is trying to put a feeling into words. He's looking at a picture of a classic "sales funnel," one that shows how the customer goes from noticing a product to buying it. If the funnel is to be believed, the path to purchase is straightforward and predictable, and the journey doesn't seem to be very fast, either. But the old models and truths of marketing have less and less to do with reality. Customers suddenly have both the power and the technology. They compare prices and features. They make demands. They ignore advertising messages and campaigns.

What's more, they have zero patience; they hate distractions and want information tailored to them, right here, right now. The funnel is so chopped up, reversed, flattened and distorted that there is nothing left to do but declare it dead. Over the funnel he writes in large letters "THE FUNNEL IS DEAD".

Philippe is a marketer and Hélène's right-hand man at American tech company EMC, one of the most powerful players in the digital revolution. He and Hélène, who has just been appointed Global Head of Marketing, are at the center of the action. They're already well aware that digitalization is changing customer behavior and that they have to do something. But the scale of it!

EMC has grown through acquisitions and now, in the early 2010s, consists of a number of silos. With each new acquisition, a new silo is added. It becomes another company within the company, with its own structure and culture. EMC's marketers sit in their own little bubbles on different continents and barely communicate with each other. Everyone has their budget, their skills, their agenda. Latin American campaigns have nothing to do with those in the Middle East, and how India deals with social media is of no concern to Japan.

And now Hélène and Philippe are sitting there with recent figures showing that two out of three customers make their purchase decisions without having been in contact with the company's sales staff. This turns everything upside down.

Philippe finds it all quite invigorating. What potential! He and Hélène set a goal: to create the world's most customer-centric, data-driven marketing organization. EMC just needs to learn how to take advantage of all the information about customers that's now available. They need to learn how to interpret it and act on it, to meet customers where they are, not where EMC is. And, most importantly, they need to break down a lot of silos and learn to truly collaborate across the organization. The logic is clear: if customers behave differently than before, a company that cares about its customers must do the same. Philippe and Hélène have realized that EMC, this giant with 60,000 employees, must fundamentally change to survive.

The first step is to present this idea to the company's 500 marketers flown in from all over the world. Philippe creates a new slide in his presentation and titles it "Organizational redesign."

1

It will soon pass

For a few years now, digital transformation has been at the top of many companies' agendas. This is not about refreshing the website, digitizing the archive, or developing a new smart app, but about something much more profound — changing the organization in such a way that it is able to make full use of the new digital technology. By now, most people have realized that technology can save a lot of time and money. Many have also come quite far in their digital maturity; not only companies but also authorities and others. The Swedish Tax Agency, which has got four out of five Swedes to file their tax returns digitally, is a brilliant example. Similarly, the Swedish Social Insurance Agency, which by 2015 had already managed to automate almost 13 million of 20 million decisions, saving 16,000 processing hours per year. Many organizations have also realized how unreasonable it is for employees to exchange thousands of files in emails every year instead of using cloud services. Or that it's questionable to continue printing and sending out informational materials, magazines, and other items that recipients only use for kindling. In the book *Att leda digital transformation* (2016), Joakim Jansson and Marie Andervin highlight the charter travel specialist.

Take Ving as an example. Not long ago, Ving distributed two and a half million travel catalogs a year. Nowadays, customers order their trips themselves online, and Ving has gone from over 50 travel agencies to just one.

It's that creating savings and efficiencies, and doing everything because customers expect it, is just not the same as using new technology to create new value. If digitalization is one thing, digital transformation is another. It's like the difference between swimming as best you can when the wave comes and surfing it.

❚❚ Many start by 'paving cow paths,' i.e., doing pretty much the same thing as before, only faster and smarter.

You use technology to save time and money. But for me, digital transformation is something much more profound, something that is fundamentally not about technology but about people. A transformation can never be a technical project that only affects a small group. It cannot reside with the IT department in isolation. Everyone has to be involved because it's a change journey for the whole organization. It has to start from the top, but it doesn't just concern a few people at the top; it concerns everyone. It is a way of life that's about seeking simplification everywhere, but also about challenging the old ways of operating. No one can sit back and think 'let them stay up there' or 'it will soon pass' — because it won't.

Change of a more traditional kind is part of everyday life in most organizations. Old IT systems are replaced by new ones, departments are merged, key people come and go, offices are rebuilt, projects are started and finished. Sometimes, there's a new law or new set of sustainability requirements, or various forms of cost savings and efficiency improvements are necessary to achieve new goals.

Such changes can be challenging enough. They can also have major consequences for those affected. But this does not necessarily mean breaking any existing norms. Kelly Odell, a Swedish- American strategy consultant, gives a good example in *Förändringshandboken* (2019): Let's say the head office is moving to another city. Selling your house and moving your whole family is no small thing. But even if an office move means major changes in the daily lives of employees, most of them can probably do their job in much the same way as before, even if it happens to be in a new environment and perhaps with new colleagues. The same goes for replacing an old IT system. The new system may take time to learn but hardly requires anyone to change their way of thinking or working in any radical sense. Odell notes that for there to be real change, where things don't go back to business as usual at the drop of a hat, people need to change their behavior. Real change is about doing things in a different way than before, leaving an old normal for a new one. And it is often much more difficult and takes much longer than you think.

❚❚ I know that I am a bit impatient as a person. If I see the need for a change, I want that change to happen quickly. But a transformation of a large established organization takes time because it may require us to rethink what is 'right' and 'what works' when it comes to running the business, building teams, recruiting, communicating, making decisions, leading — all of it! How do you actually go from being an 'ego organization' that holds its own to being an 'eco-organization' that focuses on networking and collaboration? How do you use digital technology to create something new, new value creation, new business? Then, you may not be able to rest on best practice, on the tried and tested. And you may not be able to lock yourself into the 'business case' idea, where you always want well-founded arguments for why a certain investment should be made. Because then you risk just doing what you or someone else has already done before. It's not an easy step to take — *should I make decisions on the fly?* But I think you have to take it. If you want to help your customers discover new opportunities, you have to start with yourself. You have to dare to invest in other things than you're used to so that you can become something else, something new.

Today, there is talk of a new digital business logic, of looking beyond traditional value chains to develop operations and services together with customers and suppliers in value networks. And discussion about the urgency of being able to relearn and learn anew about the importance of flexibility, speed, and innovation. This is seen as what's needed to keep up with developments, at least with some persistence. Not surprisingly, the focus is on the behaviors and attitudes of employees, on culture. Not just what people say and do, but the ideas and values behind their actions. After all, an organization is not much without the people who build it; it has no pulse of its own.

A paradigm shift

In some organizations, not least in small young tech companies, that whole fast-paced, non-hierarchical, and network-oriented innovation package is kind of built in from the start. It's in their DNA, if you will. But this is not the case in all companies, especially in larger companies where stability and control have been valued for a very long time, maybe decades.

Dismantling old structures in a large established organization is easier said than done. Or to go from all important decisions being made by a handful of people in a fancy office in central Stockholm to the power being in the data and in cross-functional, self-organizing teams. Or to go from recruiting new employees based on *competence* to recruiting based on *curiosity* or *potential*. Or to start putting the principle of *learning most* before *knowing best*. Not to mention abandoning the principle of *winning through competition* for the principle of *winning through collaboration*.

Where do you start? How should it be measured? Will it ever be finished? And how the heck will it be communicated? It's not hard to see the problem with the message: "Well, everyone, we need to be more innovative. So we thought we'd try 50% structure, 50% chaos. You know, like Google. Any questions on that?"

> **❚❚** Many people are now being told, 'You have to think new, you have to come up with more new ideas,' but then the same old structures and management systems remain in place and the same behaviors are rewarded that were rewarded in the past. I'm thinking about perceived control. I think we sometimes confuse a sense of control with actual control. It's so easy to think that you have control just because you have clear policies or steering committees for everything or have control over your employees down to the smallest detail and have clear, measurable goals. Or because you break down key figures into perfect columns that do not overlap and because everything comes together nicely at the end. But I think that form of control can be limiting in a transformative

4

stage. Then, maybe we need to let go of the reins and show a little more trust. Perhaps we don't just have to have completely new metrics but have to accept a structure that doesn't quite fit. Maybe we can't or shouldn't have a grip on everything.

In some organizations, the behavioral change required can be so extensive that it is in practice about changing the entire culture — here, a digital and a cultural transformation go hand in hand. But if experience shows that it's surprisingly difficult to get 30 employees to switch to an activity-based way of working, then what does it take for a large established organization to succeed with a paradigm shift of the kind we are talking about here? How do you get hundreds of employees, perhaps thousands, to change their attitude to what can and should happen at work?

Fortunately, many people have already asked this question. Some have also come a long way in the search for an answer.

Four key conditions

Back in 2003, long before anyone put digital transformation at the top of the agenda, the McKinsey report *The psychology of change management* concluded that employees will change their mind-set, their approach, only if:

- They see the purpose of the change and think that point is important — at least important enough to try it.
- They have the skills they need to do what is required.
- They see people they respect walk the talk.
- The surrounding structures (e.g., reward systems) support the new behavior.

It is the *combination of* these four factors that's needed to bring about a change in behavior and attitude — a change in culture. In other words, it's not enough to change the "hard" things that can be touched, such as redrawing the organizational chart or moving to bright, fresh premises. Nor will you achieve a lasting change in behavior just by inviting all employees to a rousing kick-off. Or by hiring the world's most expensive consultants.

5

It's not enough to give the right people the right resources or create well-thought-out plans that are impeccably implemented.

The "softer" aspects of change management cannot be ignored. For example, the importance of leaders who show the way in word and deed cannot be underestimated. And there is no getting around the question of why. Why should I change? The employee that doesn't want to change their behavior will not do so, no matter how hard a person tries.

What the four points above really say is that, in order to change their attitude, people must be willing and able to do so. An organization that does not consider these two musts during a change journey simply does not stand a chance. Every organization is different, and cultural change may not always be necessary. But right now, our society and the conditions for many companies are fundamentally changing. Digitalization is not the only force in this development, but it is an extremely strong one. There is talk of exponential development. It's quite slow in the beginning: $1 + 1 = 2$, then $2 + 2 = 4$, and so on.

Manageable and harmless. But it goes faster and faster, and suddenly the initially modest curve rises straight up. On top of that, we get a lot of friction between a new reality and the old way of organizing ourselves that's adapted to a more linear development.

At the same time, there is something inspiring and hopeful about what's happening. There are dizzying new opportunities to change things for the better, both in our workplaces and in society at large. "Business as usual" will soon be neither possible nor desirable.

So if we want to create a more flexible, responsive, innovative, and agile organization — where do we find the energy to get that ball rolling?

> **❚❚** I came from EMC, one of America's most customer-oriented companies. The letters E, M, and C are actually the founders' initials, but the CEO used to say that they stood for 'Everybody Meets the Customer.' He meant that everyone in the organization meets the customer, that it matters what everyone does, because everyone affects the customer's experience of the company as a whole. At EMC, the customer was everything. The entire organization was built around the customer. No one got up and went home

at five o'clock if a customer had a problem; people worked all night if necessary. Nobody talked about 'customer obsession,' either. It didn't serve any purpose because the customers' needs and wishes were already everything. When I arrived at Telia, it was something of a culture shock. Telia has long been a very technology-oriented company, one with a completely different history and culture than EMC and in a completely different industry. I felt that we had to talk about the customer in a new way and start thinking about the customer in everything we do. This didn't need to be communicated at EMC, but it was at Telia. But nothing happens just because I stand on a stage and say, 'Let's take care of the customer.' So in the early days, I traveled to all our offices around Sweden. I asked to start each visit in one of the shops, so that it would be the first thing I did in the morning. I wanted to meet customers, see the store, and talk first with those who work closest to the customers. If I started in the office, it would immediately be an inside-out perspective.

Customer obsession

"Customer focus" must be one of the most popular values in the world. Sometimes there's talk of putting the customer first or foremost, even of loving the customer. Then, this message — *customer centricity* — is communicated everywhere. And who can argue with that? Most people realize that customers are important, because without them we may as well turn off the lights and go home. But to go from that to living a true "customer focus" in practice, every day, can be quite a leap.

Customer focus only becomes interesting when it's taken seriously. Like when the CEO starts every meeting by talking about the customer and doesn't simply push customer problems onto the sales manager but takes responsibility and gets up and leaves a meeting with the group management if that's what it takes — *because the customer comes first*. Or when customer satisfaction starts to be measured in a new way, moved up the KPI hierarchy, and linked to employee bonuses. Or when you cover the cost of letting some employees work at night if it makes things easier for them and for customers, even though you know it won't increase sales. Or when a question like "What do customers think of this?" or "Will this change really be better for the customers?" is the first question asked in the room, not the third or fifth. Or when the management team is out working in the store or working in customer service. Or when the leaders at the top talk about "customer obsession" and also live by their words.

Then, things can happen.

If customer obsession is enforced in practice, from the highest level down through every part of the organization, most things are impacted. Because then a hunt begins — first for everything that bothers the customer, then for everything that would make life easier for the customer, and then for anything that could be of value to the customer.

> ❙❙ Ninety-five percent of all good ideas come not from the top, but from people further out in the organization. Let's say someone working at a store in a mall thinks, 'We should open at 11:00 instead of 9:00 and stay open longer in the evenings so that customers can come after work.' This is not the sort of thing they would take up with management or even with their line manager. They might think, 'I can't change that' or 'It's someone else's responsibility.' Or they may think that it's unimportant. But those ideas, the many small, smart ideas, can combine to have a huge impact on the customer experience. I think those ideas can come more easily if the CEO and the management are constantly talking about the customer and are out there themselves working in stores or showing in other ways that the customer is our top focus. Then, the ideas are somehow legitimized, they are encouraged, and we create a kind of customer obsession movement.

That there is such energy in the idea of customer obsession is largely due to its creative power — because putting customer obsession into practice raises questions all over the place. Can we make what we do smoother, better, simpler, and more personalized? Do we have the data to show that we're spending time and effort on the right thing, that this really has value for the customer? What in our way of working isn't really adapted to the customers' needs but to our own?

> **❚❚** I want to know — what are the 'root causes' of customers not loving us? What are the top five customer frustrations, and what is actually causing them? Then, you might realize that what creates problems for customers is that your own organization looks the way it does. EMC was completely customer-focused but had grown through acquisitions, and that extremely rapid expansion had created a lot of silos. Everyone put the customer first, but within their own silo. There was no real sense that *we were in this together*, nor was there any really strong collaboration across the organization. This meant that the right hand sometimes didn't know what the left hand was doing. Two or even three people from EMC could unexpectedly bump into each other at the same customer site if the customer had called and asked to discuss several different issues at once, such as both storage and security: "What, are you also from EMC? Will you be at the meeting too?" This is hugely disruptive for a customer. The customer is not 'divided' just because the organization is divided into a lot of different silos, each one only aware of its own business.
>
> It was the same at Telia if we go back a few years. For example, if a customer wanted to have wifi at home, someone came and installed the fiber. But if for some reason it didn't work when they went to connect — because the apartment was too big, for example — then it wasn't the responsibility of the installers to handle it because they were their own organization. In that case, the customer had to call another number to get help from customer service. But it's not the customer who should suffer because an organization's own structure looks the way it does. I believe

that it's very important in a transformation not to get stuck in making changes to increase efficiency from your own perspective and your own structures and processes, but from the customer's perspective.

The energy behind the idea of customer obsession is also due to the fact that any individual employee can quite easily make the concept their own. "Customer obsession" can be understood and embraced on so many different levels. Compared to other common value words, such as "quality," "responsibility," "development," or "openness," every employee can easily imagine how customer obsession can be applied in everyday life. It's possible to put on "customer obsession glasses" if you like. In its simplest form, it can be about having more generous opening hours, transferring customers from an old system to a more flexible e-service, or making it possible to fill out certain forms online. In its more complex form, it can be about initiating a deeper cultural change and reinvigorating the entire organization to create the best possible conditions for innovation.

> **❚❚** We gathered Telia's 300 top managers for a workshop, a 'boost,' to drive change. We did exercises where the participants had to solve problems themselves by trying out a possible solution, creating a prototype, testing it, and then either rejecting it or developing it further, all at high speed. It was about understanding what exploratory leadership is all about. What does more agile decision-making look like, when you don't wait for a big meeting in two months and don't appoint a new steering committee, but instead run your business decisions in sprints and have short, iterative meetings with those who are most crucial to help arrive at the right decision? I think this was an important moment, something many people needed to practice. What do you do when you move from the straightforward linear approach and delivering on a target goal to working more dynamically? And working with a more customer-based approach? Because if you work based on the customer, then you test things.

True "customer obsession" is about doing business, but in a fun way. It can be an immensely powerful springboard for change because it's so closely linked to exploration and innovation. Because those who are truly customer obsessed are not content with giving the customer what they want — they strive to give the customer what they don't yet know they want. And not only that, but striving, by extension, to build something meaningful and make the world a little better. Because when we have scrapped the old systems and sped up and streamlined and simplified, then we can step up a notch. From that height, the view is different. We can ask a different kind of question: Can we add value, can we create something different, something new?

And, leading into the next chapter, what does it take to actually do that?

O n a small raised stage in a conference room at Telia's head office in Solna, Sweden, Magnus Grönblad stands looking out over 150 of the company's top managers. It's a strangely thick atmosphere in the room.

Magnus will hold a workshop on self-leadership. He starts with the basics. He talks about self-esteem, about what it means to believe in your own value regardless of your performance. He also talks about the danger of confusing self-esteem with self- confidence. "Then I *am* what I *do*, I become my achievements. And that's fine as long as I'm perfect." He pauses for a moment and turns directly to the audience. "How many of you in here feel that you are perfect?" An occasional hand goes up. Scattered giggles. "And", he continues, "if I then get feedback, for example on a report I have submitted, and receive criticism, I can find it very difficult to take that criticism in a constructive way. Because if I *am* my performance, I *am the* report, then I may feel that I'm being personally attacked and need to defend myself. I blame myself or close myself off and mentally beat myself up. Or I learn to avoid all situations where I risk making mistakes ad being questioned or criticized. I start making decisions based on fear."

He hardly needs to state that all these outcomes would be very unfortunate for an organization that strives to be more courageous and innovative.

Then, Magnus talks about why self-leadership is so important in our time. "The world we live in will only change faster and faster and become more complex, mobile, ambiguous, and unpredictable. And so we need to know the answer to some fundamental questions in order not to lose our footing: What am I personally striving for? What is my purpose? Which values are important to me, and do I live in accordance with them? What drives me? Why am I working here, in this role, right now?"

The managers in the room are used to talking about revenue pressures, KPIs, structural costs, differentiation, and legacy systems. They are not as used to someone turning to them and asking straight out: "What are your personal values? Who do you want to be? And why do you work here at Telia?"

The strangely intimate atmosphere is reinforced by each member of the management team answering that final question in front of the whole assembly: "Why am I here?" Some executives have devoted half their lives to the company but have never spoken about it to anyone, let alone to so many people at once. As they take the small stage, an expectant silence spreads through the room; you can hear a pin drop. Suddenly, it's not a manager, a role, a name, standing there talking, but a flesh and blood human being. It becomes unexpectedly personal.

During a break, Hélène goes up to Magnus and says, "I want you to be "in my face" with these issues from now on, for you to drive this work in the organization. Because this, Magnus, this is *exactly* what we need."

2

Why am I here?

In a small entrepreneurial company, the culture is often strong. The manager, perhaps a committed founder, is visible and involved, and everyone knows what they stand for and strive for. Employees can then quite easily decide which decision or behavior is "right," based on the goals that are set.

In large established companies, the complexity is different. The dedicated founder, if there was one, is long gone. Others have been hired and have, in turn, hired others. There is always a culture of some kind, of course, but it may not be explicit, conscious, or shared. It doesn't act as the glue or serve as a compass in everyday life, and it doesn't give anyone an extra bounce in their step. Out of 5,000 or 20,000 employees, perhaps only half, if that, care about the arrival of a new CEO or read what the website says about the company's vision or mission statement or core values. Getting everyone to act day to day in a way that contributes towards the goals can be a challenge, to say the least.

One way to deal with this is to manage employees through clear rules and instructions, with a focus on measurable objectives and rigorous supervision. This may not have been the case from the outset, but perhaps the business has grown slowly, over decades or more, adding one process, policy, and pointer after another. Then, as competition and complexity increase both internally and externally, the screws are tightened further. More governance. More control. More instructions and guidelines. More administration and documentation.

It can be too much of a good thing. You end up in an impressive fortress with inner walls a meter thick. Adjusting a stone or two is out of the question, or else the whole building could collapse. Not to mention knocking out a wall to open up a couple rooms. And then one day, employees no longer believe that what goes on in another room or on another floor is any of their business. Suddenly, they spend half their time reporting things. They're controlled in every way and do only as they're told. The stovepipe mentality spreads, inefficiency increases, and frustration grows.

If those of us in a large established company want to regain some of the resilience of youth, or even reinvent ourselves and start again, we'll have to replace micromanagement with something else.

Something to lean on

So if frameworks, rules, and bureaucracy can't hold a large organization together and steer it in the right direction — what could do the job?

A growing number of companies see a higher purpose and a strong set of values as a possible answer to that question. With a good grasp of the core of the business, what we do and why, and the principles that guide us along the way, we can let go of some control. They'll be something to hold on to when things go wrong. Studies also show that values-driven organizations are more profitable and have higher growth rates. They're more willing to change, are better at collaboration, and have more satisfied customers. They are also more attractive as employers — now that we, especially younger generations, increasingly identify with our jobs. Deloitte's *Millennial survey* (2018) of 10,000 people born between 1983 and 1994, known as Millennials or Generation Y, shows that they want to work for companies that don't just donate money to charity every year, but where the whole business feels meaningful and contributes to the betterment of society on a deeper level.

In short, having a good answer to the "why" question is becoming increasingly important. Why are we doing this? Why should we embark on this journey? What is the point?

> **❚❚** When I joined EMC, the strategy was being redesigned with a focus on cloud services, big data, and data security. This was in 2009. and I'd never heard of these things before. It was so forward-looking, and people were super excited to be on that journey. In addition, there were financial resources to make the dream come true. EMC could buy a lot of exciting companies, and there was a lot of momentum in the organization. A high pace and an insane amount of work, but also a lot of fun. There wasn't much

talk about EMC's 'culture,' but there certainly was one. There was a pronounced customer focus, and EMC was extremely forward-leaning, no one ever leaned back. The company's CEO, Joe Tucci, was also a very important person in the organization. He was a relationship person. He had the ability to empower people, to make them grow in a way that they might not have with another leader. That created a kind of culture of loyalty around him. So a few years went by, and we had delivered on the strategy, and the company was doing fantastically well. But then, Joe started talking about retirement, and something changed. There was confusion in the organization. We just felt, what happens now? Not only was it getting to be time for EMC to take the next step and further develop their strategy, but now perhaps the most important person in the company was planning to leave. Suddenly, it became quite obvious to me that there was no shared higher purpose at EMC. There was nothing to *lean on*. What if you had said, for example, 'We see a world that is going to be incredibly vulnerable in terms of data integrity and personal data, so because we're so good at security, we're going to take a bigger role in defending democracy'? Then, people might not have felt so lost. Then, that purpose would have become *superior* to the fact of who was the boss or to making money. But now, there was no such thing. It wasn't long before EMC was acquired by Dell. I think that became the solution.

A poor answer to the "why" question makes the organization vulnerable. "To make more money" becomes problematic when more and more customers base their choices on how they believe a company impacts society, the environment, and people's everyday lives, and when more and more young people are attracted to employers with an inspiring mission and vision. And if you're already making a lot of money, how excited are you by the prospect of making even more? Moreover, if the existing business is pretty darned profitable, why "attack" it and go for something new? And will the answer "to make more money" really point us in the right direction when we reach another fork in the road and have to make quick decisions?

In short, "to make more money" may be an answer that's easy to understand and seductive in its simplicity, but it's not a good guide.

Fortunately, there are many fun and inspiring answers to the "why" question that far surpass "to make more money than last year." For example, those that touch on the themes of *exploring* (new products, markets, etc.), *surpassing oneself* (in areas other than profitability), or *helping* (improving people's lives in some way). IKEA's "To create a better everyday life for the many people" is one of the world's most famous answers to the why-are-we-really-doing-this question. Or take Google, who wants to "organize the world's information and make it universally accessible and useful." Or Microsoft: "Our mission is to empower every person and every organization on the planet to achieve more." A good answer to the "why" question can speak to our hearts and awaken our humanity. Maybe it can even shine like a giant arrow at our feet — *this is where we're going!* And of course, pursuing your purpose and doing it well will result in financial returns, an obvious prerequisite for sustainable business.

> ❚❚ When I joined the group management at Telia, we set the purpose for the whole company as 'Bringing the world closer — on the consumers' terms.' It was another way of saying that it's not enough to maximize sales in our networks, but that we need to think beyond that, broader, more innovative. How important are landlines to you today compared to ten years ago? Most likely not nearly as important. But how important will e-health be to you in five years? Probably very important. Especially if you live in the countryside and don't have a clinic as your nearest neighbor. And it's not just Telia that does things that matter to people, but many other players. In other words, this means that companies must start looking for new partnerships. Who can you work with to deliver on what's relevant for the customers when expectations change with the times?

If you create a company with the goal of selling within five years, then maybe you can think differently, but if you want to grow in the longer term, then I think you have to have an overarching purpose that's so well-anchored in the organization that you can talk about it as a culture. Because you'll go down one path and start building something, but then some new technology or new competitor or whatever else comes along that upends or changes everything, and then you have to build on the next path, and the next path. If you don't live and breathe that culture when you constantly have to find new ways forward, when you have to drive so many different parallel changes, I think it will be very difficult. It will also be difficult to retain staff because I think people want to be on a *journey*.

Trust in common sense

Values-based leadership is about employees feeling so confident in where the organization is headed and in what its leaders stand for that they can make the right decisions in critical everyday situations — "how should I handle this?" — without turning to a manager to ask if they're doing the right thing.

On a deeper level, it's about having and signaling trust in *the common sense of your employees.*

A study by the American consulting firm Bain & Company shows that companies such as Apple, Netflix, Google, and Dell, which are 40% more productive than the average company, deliberately avoid creating processes where employees spend their time and energy on things that don't actually create value. For example, processes tied to budgeting; processes that involve administration, control, and evaluation; or processes to ensure that no one takes too long at lunch, uses their working hours to surf, works at the wrong time or in the wrong place, or expenses an overly pricy dinner on a business trip. Because while it's bad if employees misbehave, it's worse to suggest that they are not trustworthy adults. And how productive is it to explain every single receipt, fill in timesheets, or approve snack expenses? Whereas much have changed in the tech sector during the past years, the truth about keeping focus on processes that support common sense and not controlling every single detail – is an important aspect both for efficiencies and building the culture.

> **"** If our goal is to create value, then we need to ask ourselves how we can best use our time. How much time should we as an organization spend checking that employees are doing what they're supposed to? And just as importantly, how much time should I as a leader spend on that? In the first months of a new job, I'm into everything. I go to every meeting I'm invited to, and I get involved in all possible contexts to get the best possible overview of the organization. But then I think it's important to step back. I have a goal for myself that I call the 50/30/20 rule. I want to spend a maximum of 20% of my time on internal governance and follow-ups. Then, I want to spend 30% working with the teams, creating value together and helping us move forward. The rest of my time, preferably half, I want to spend externally: meeting customers, partners, stakeholders in the ecosystem. And of course making sure to visit the different countries and offices. These meetings are extremely valuable to stay close to the business and what drives it — and it always offers new insights and, crucially, keeps you in learning mode. This is the foundation that ensures I stay in touch with the outside world and what's happening in the relevant industries and therefore helps me to stay clear on how I can contribute in the best possible way.

Walk the talk

A company that doesn't have a solid set of values may start by engaging a consultant or an agency to help identify the values that most of the organization can subscribe to. Of course, you ask your employees what they think. "Do we stand for 'respect'? Or maybe more 'openness'?" In the next step, you describe how these values should be used in daily work through concrete behaviors, and then you write the values in capital letters on the website, print them on posters, coffee mugs, and t-shirts, and run some seminars and a workshop. A year later, most employees know that the organization has values, but when asked directly, they still stumble over the answer. "Our values? They are 'transparency', 'sustainability' and... well, something else." Even if they can recite them in their sleep, the words may not have an impact in the real world. The gap between values and reality can be very wide.

So, again, how do you do it? Most people who have explored this question come to the same conclusion. You just *do*.

It starts at the top, with the CEO and the management team walking the talk. Not just for a month or two, or for a few decisions, but all the time, every day. Does it say "sustainability" on the website, on posters, and on coffee mugs, but employee after employee burns out? Does it say "responsibility," but no one checks the working conditions of subcontractors? Does it say "curiosity," but everything is based on best practices and repeating what others have already done?

That balloon will soon deflate.

There are many examples of large and successful organizations with strong cultures and values — IKEA and Virgin — so it's certainly possible to succeed. There are also organizations that succeed well in the times of growth and prosperity but fail miserably during more challenging times. This is not least the case within the tech sector.

All evidence suggests that it's impossible to succeed if those who are supposed to lead the way behave in a manner that's inconsistent with these values. Or if they don't reward and encourage behaviors that are said to be desirable on paper, or don't put their foot down and question behaviors that are incompatible with the direction they've set and the movement they want to see. Someone once said, "If you want to understand the culture of a company, look at what is rewarded and punished."

❚❚ During my very first days at Telia, I sat in lots of meetings. No matter what question I asked, it was answered by showing a PowerPoint. Even if I only asked

23

ten fairly straightforward questions, they could easily have put together 95 slides so as not to risk answering without one. One of Telia's values is 'dare,' and another is 'simplify.' I quickly felt, *this is not working*. So I said, 'From now on, nobody can come into the room with a PowerPoint. You can do whatever else you want — you can write a memo, draw on the whiteboard, whatever — but no PowerPoints.'

The importance of what the organization's leaders do is also encouraging. It means that even a small symbolic act can have a big impact. One of the main messages of this book is the immense importance of leaders acting as role models, not just talking the talk but walking the walk. We will return to this issue later in the book.

My true north — and ours

If one side of the coin is the organization's (collective) purpose and values, then the other is each individual's own personal purpose and values. Anyone who reads books on leadership and change will sooner or later come across Edward Deci and Richard Ryan's research on motivation, on what makes people feel their own inner drive. Deci and Ryan, both professors of psychology at the University of Rochester in New York, have shown that external rewards such as money or benefits are no match for the experience of doing something that we want to do and that feels meaningful and enjoyable. When we do something that feels like a *reward in itself*, we feel better and perform better.

❚❚ I don't believe in pushing values from above. The motivation that comes from within is much more powerful. If I find my own 'why,' I become involved in a completely different way because then I'm doing something of my own free will. I think it's important for leaders to think about these issues for themselves and encourage others to do the same. If I do something because I really want to, because it feels right and important to me personally, then the work itself can energize me. On the other hand, if I haven't found my own personal 'why' and I 'just keep on working,' I think it will be very difficult to make it in the long run. Especially when the demands are constantly growing and both the pace of change and level of uncertainty increase. Standing in front of others and telling them why I work here, right now, in this role, at this company, is also a commitment, something I want to live up to. It's a way of saying that *I choose to be part of this journey.*

Self-leadership is just another word for something we do most of the time: we direct our thoughts and behaviors towards goals. But we do it more or less effectively and more or less consciously. We don't always know what we truly think is important or where we're going. The compass needle points here and there. This uncertainty is not what we need when the storm is at its worst. Most people recognize the value of getting to know themselves better, and no one wants to take a back seat in their own life. But for self-leadership to become more than a private matter, "I want" must be linked to "we want." The point is that everyone should be pulling in the same direction. And then the organization needs to have a good answer to the "why" question and to have identified the values that will point the way. Otherwise, how will individual employees be able to see how their own purpose, values, and objectives align with those of the group?

Some organizations are characterized by strong values and an attractive vision, and they focus heavily on recruiting the "right" people — not only competent employees, but those who are sincerely passionate about what the company does and stands for. Google has traditionally fallen into this category, for instance. But most organizations are not Google. Most organizations are not made up of a certain "breed" of people, but of individuals with all manner of qualities and motivations and personal goals, not all of whom necessarily think the job is reward enough in itself. Larger established companies may also have a long legacy of cultural norms to deal with, some of which may be embedded in the walls themselves. In such an organization, you don't succeed with a cultural transformation by occasionally hiring someone whom you think has the right drive and the right values. It's far too slow. You have to work with your teams, and do it now. Here, it's absolutely necessary to communicate — almost *demonstrate* — the purpose and values of the organization, and it's crucial that the leaders practice what they preach. It's also very important not only to talk about the importance of leading oneself, but to actually give employees the tools and space to do this in practice.

> **"** In an established organization, there may be a lot that needs to change in order for self-leadership to fully function. In practice, this may mean that employees must be given greater freedom than before to manage their time and work. They may have to take more responsibility and make their own decisions more often, but also start communicating more about those decisions, get more frequent coaching, and invite more people into the earlier stages of the process — long before it ends up with a steering committee. They may have to both give and receive feedback, not just once a month or once a year, but on an ongoing basis. What worked well today, and what can we learn from it? How effective have we been? How much fun have we had? Perhaps they need to be challenged to get to know themselves better, but also to get to know each other, because otherwise it's difficult to put the right team together and build realtrust in each other. And managers certainly need to take a step back and take more of a coaching approach.

In other words, the step from micromanagement to self-leadership can be quite a large one. Self-leadership requires cooperation, communication, and transparency. And not least — trust. Anyone who takes a peek at how things actually look internally, how the organization is structured, how people usually work, what's rewarded, how employees are monitored, etc., will probably discover that a lot of these things are based on completely different principles.

Want to join the journey?

The kind of change we're talking about here — a paradigm shift — can be quite painful. There may be talk of breaking down silos, of self-leadership and continuous feedback and evaluation, of activity-based ways of working, cross-functional teams and zero tolerance for PowerPoints. There may be a group that spontaneously feels *This is not for me* and decides to drop out. Others may feel overwhelmed by yet another change initiative that they had no say in. Some may worry about not being enough or not fitting in, wondering *how do they really expect me to work?* There may also be some who are afraid of losing their job. Because what is the manager's role in all this? If everyone manages themselves, do we need managers at all?

The aforementioned duo Deci and Ryan have tried to identify what it takes for people to feel that powerful sense of inner motivation. For example, the desire to work hard to realize a vision or the desire to be part of a transformative journey of change. They have summarized their ideas in a theory that's become widely accepted, the so-called self-determination theory. Deci and Ryan, and hundreds of other researchers in their wake, have found three things that are particularly important for our intrinsic motivation. In simplified terms, we need to (1) feel competent, like "we can do this"; (2) feel that we're reasonably free to make decisions and influence things in our own everyday lives; and (3) feel a sense of belonging or affinity with our group and society at large.

If the theory is correct, we should perhaps stop thinking about trying to motivate others and start thinking about how we can ensure that these three needs are met so that others can feel their own inner motivation.

> In many organizations, and especially in large established companies, there may be an 'immune system.' It rarely lies with the employees at the top who are part of identifying the change. And especially not with those who meet customers on a daily basis, where they're often super enthusiastic when you come and talk about change and customer focus and self-leadership. *Finally, this is happening!* The immune defense is not there, closest to the customer, nor is it with the most senior managers, but

somewhere in between. Perhaps it's not a single person who shows resistance, but many — even though they've had many meetings together and think that they've been invited and that everyone has been involved. But it's not really that strange. The resistance is at the level of those colleagues who have the most to lose, or at least feel that way. Those who wonder, what happens to my department, my responsibilities, my budget, my team, my role? The change affects them with full force in their daily work. I've learned one important thing from the change processes that I've been involved in, and that is not to underestimate the resistance that may exist deeper into an organization. I think you may need to put more focus there, to be humbler in the face of that challenge. What do they need to be willing and able to participate?

Employee obsession

In the book *Get digital or die trying* (2016), Arash Gilan and Jonas Hammarberg state that everything that can be digitalized will be digitized, that everything that can be digitalized can be copied, and that everything that can be copied will therefore decrease in value. This may sound gloomy, but it depends on how you look at it. Because it looks all the brighter for everything that remains, beyond the ones and zeros. For things that — at least so far — distinguish us humans from robots. Like imagination, compassion, values, ethics, morals, creativity, and intuition.

The connection between digital transformation and deep customer insight is obvious. But is there perhaps a corresponding link between transformation and deep insight into employees? If customer focus is one possible springboard for transformation, is employee focus another? If there is anything technology can help us with, it's to create more space for us humans to do what we do best.

When and how can we make use of digital technologies to bring out the best in people and not reduce them to robots? If we put on those glasses, we will discover opportunities everywhere. We can start soft, open new doors, in any business. Should the staff in a grocery store sit hunched over a conveyor belt for hours and blip items, or should customers scan their own items and check themselves out? Should a receptionist type in the names of people coming and going, or should visitors register themselves on a computer? Should a pathologist or radiologist assess x-rays when a computer can do the job just as well? These questions, which someone raised many years ago, are being answered today.

Other questions are more recent but equally interesting: should an HR specialist plough through hundreds of CVs and cover letters and then make their own assessment, or can a computer make a fairer selection? Should an economist spend time on forecasting, or should AI do it? Should a manager make decisions, plan, prioritize, administer, verify, and follow up, or can a high-functioning team do just as well as long as they have access to sufficiently high-quality data?

Today, enormous resources are devoted to getting to know customers better, to understanding their needs, wishes, histories, motivations, values, and future desires. What do customers want and need, today and tomorrow? What would help them save a few minutes here and there? What would make their everyday life easier, more fun, and more rewarding?

> **▐▐** There are few organizations that have a one-sided customer focus, but the vast majority also invest in employees in various ways. And it's not possible to become customer obsessed if employees don't feel seen, respected, motivated, and involved and can have fun and feel good about their situation. But I think we're entering an era where employees and corporate culture are more important than anything else, where culture is the only thing that cannot be copied, the only thing that's unique. Today, we talk a lot about the customer journey and the customer experience. I think we need to start talking at least as much about the employee journey and the employee experience. I think we need to become 'employee obsessed.'

Most people have heard that employees are a company's most important resource; this message is communicated everywhere. What if it's now, with the fourth industrial revolution, in a fast-changing, unpredictable, globalized, digitalized world, that it's taken seriously?

According to the Foundation for Strategic Research, one in two jobs will be automated within 20 years. Accounting assistants, cashiers, and machine operators are among the most vulnerable, with computers predicted to take over with more than 95% probability. Things look better for anyone whose job requires social skills, originality, artistry, dexterity, concern for others, and the ability to negotiate and persuade (though not necessarily all at once). Among those least likely to be replaced by computers are teachers, hairdressers, psychologists, and architects. So far, robots are failing there.

One can choose to focus either on all the challenges that come with such developments or on the opportunities that arise. A hopeful person sees how, in the near future, computers/robots/AI will take care of the most exhausting and soul-destroying tasks so that we humans can focus on being there for each other and creating new value together.

As in the case of "customer obsession," a genuine "employee obsession" can be the start of an exciting hunt. First, for monotonous and time-consuming tasks where employees are not using their skills. Then, for anything that would make it easier for them to do their jobs and take greater responsibility and initiative. Then, for anything that could further increase their skills and commitment and strengthen their ability to rethink and innovate.

> The self-leadership seed planted at Telia a few years ago grew into something big, a whole movement. Telia developed a self-leadership program for all employees throughout the group. Everyone who wanted to could spend working hours exploring their own purpose, values, and motivations and how these could be linked to everyday tasks. I see self-leadership as an important part of the change journey because it's the opposite of micromanagement. And if you learn how to lead yourself, you don't want to go back in time.

In an organization focused on minimizing the waste of human resources, a platform for more profound change will soon take shape. Because even if we start with the question, "Can a computer do this so I don't have to?" we can ask ourselves bolder questions in the next stage: what can make us more engaged and motivated than we are today, and how can we feel more "flow" at work? How can we learn more and faster? What could make us stronger as individuals and as a team? Braver, more innovative? In short, what prevents us from reaching our full potential?

If there's enormous energy in "customer obsession," there's a corresponding energy in "employee obsession." Because who doesn't want to become their best self at work?

3

Guy Janssens has brought a rug from his office in Antwerp, Belgium. The rug, round and colorful, now lies in the middle of the floor in a meeting room at a conference center on the outskirts of Stockholm. Around the rug stand Hélène and the closest members of her management team. Some know each other well, but most are new to the job and to their roles. They know very little about each other. A few months earlier, when Hélène had just taken over as CEO, she had called Guy: "In August, 10 out of 14 people in the old management team will no longer be in their roles. In September, I'll start recruiting new people. In December, we'll be 14 people in the group again. But we don't know each other. I want you to come here and help us build a team. You'll have two days."

Now, a few months later, Guy has a pretty clear picture of who's standing around the rug. The members of the new management group have already answered a whole battery of questions about themselves, what they think is important, how they see themselves, etc., and Guy has then talked through the answers with each of them over the phone. Sometimes, the conversation lasted an hour or more. Using the Lumina Spark personality test, he has created a profile or "portrait" of each person in the group. It takes the form of a colorful mandala, different for each person. As in other tests, there are no clear boundaries between yellow, blue, red, and green; the colors flow into each other. No one is labeled as a cautious, detail-oriented, introverted "blue person" or an enthusiastic, charming, outgoing "yellow person." The picture that emerges is more complex than that. This test is designed to go beyond such stereotypes. After all, most people have all colors in them. Moreover, it's one thing how we behave in private and quite another thing how we behave at work, when we have to cooperate with others in a group.

Sometimes, we also go to extremes in our behavior, pushing it a little extra in one direction or another, especially if we're in a hurry or feeling stressed or insecure.

Guy turns to Hélène and says, without warning, "Can you tell me why these people are in this room right now? You're the one who chose them." Hélène is taken aback and has to collect her thoughts. But what she then says about each of them — the whole thing takes almost half an hour — is therefore not so prepared and rehearsed, but comes spontaneously and from the heart.

Hélène is then invited to sit on a chair in the center of the circle. Guy asks each person in the management group to, one at a time, stand on the color of the rug (or rather mix of colors) where they think Hélène feels most at home and also to explain to her and the others why they've stood there. Interestingly, almost no one stands in the same place on the rug as anyone else. Everyone has different images of Hélène, everyone sees different aspects.

When they've gone around the team, Guy asks if anyone else in the group would like to take the chair in the middle of the circle. Everyone does. Guy says, "But... it's going to take the whole two days that we have, do you realize that?" Everyone wants to do it anyway.

Afterwards, someone in the group tells Hélène that it was the first time he had received that kind of feedback in his entire life.

3

No more people like you

Competition is increasing in our globalized, digitalized world. And yet another word, a word with the opposite meaning, shines bright like a star over the entire digital revolution.

Collaboration.

Alone is not strong in a connected world. Nor is it the fastest or the smartest. This is the age of networks and relationships. New ecosystems. Keeping to yourself has become obsolete, and now we have to share knowledge, thoughts, ideas. Preferably also cars, summer cottages, and screwdrivers. Instead of owning and accumulating, we will rent, donate, exchange, and borrow. On Facebook, LinkedIn, Instagram, YouTube, Twitter, and Snapchat, we extend our tentacles in all directions, creating new constellations and making connections everywhere. We air our opinions like never before and publish our objectives, motives, plans, strategies, and figures. If we're unusually good at anything in particular, then we share that knowledge for free, convinced that we'll ultimately benefit from it.

In the labor market, too, we see a different kind of mobility and networking than before. Employees in Sweden are changing jobs more often, with fewer permanent positions and more fixed-term assignments. There's talk of "the new flexible labor market," about a growing gig economy with more and more freelancers and consultants offering their skills on a temporary basis and then moving on. Young people build their CVs not by being loyal and slowly climbing the ladder within the same company, but by changing jobs frequently, preferably every two or three years, and purposefully accumulating experience, employers, and contacts.

And today's organizations don't look like yesterday's, either. This is the age of blurred boundaries and complex interdependencies. Production is now in India, the customer in Italy, the subcontractor in China, and the owners scattered around the world. Employees, too, are scattered all over the place; they work partly from home, come from different parts of the world, and, as previously mentioned, are not always employees at all but self-employed people who come in and work on specific projects. And the former competitor in the neighboring country may even have become a partner.

People in today's world, especially younger generations, are also more fickle, impatient, demanding, and values-driven than in the past, both as consumers and employees. We want to continue developing at work, not just to get better at what we do, but to grow as people. We don't want to be fed tasks — *do this* — but to work on our own projects and shape both our tasks and our processes based on our specific talents and personal needs. We're also constantly connected and ready to evaluate and rate everything that comes our way. Not just gadgets, but brands and employers, right down to individual professionals. Soon, there won't be a CEO, advertising campaign, website, office space, logo, chatbot, recruitment process, or HR manager that we can't reward with a "like" or rate out of five stars.

Overjoyed to finally have our say, we also rate other people's ratings.

So it goes in the age of digital services companies. What does all this mean for an organization that wants to be an unbeatable combination of "customer obsessed" and "employee obsessed," that wants to surf this huge swift wave of collaboration?

Moving out there — static in here

Firstly, as we've already discussed in previous chapters, it's important that an organization's ambitions to bring about change are not stifled by its structure and culture. If it is moving and changing in the outside world, it cannot stay stagnant internally. Silo structures, a lack of communication and common goals, and other various boundaries can make the organization inefficient, inflexible, and "non-innovative." With meter-thick walls between the different rooms of the fortress (departments, professions, etc.), it can be difficult to see the big picture and focus on what actually creates value and matters to customers. If the culture doesn't encourage collaboration across boundaries, but rather safeguards one's own competence, expertise, responsibilities, and financial rewards, then decision-making can be slow.

It can be uncomfortable, or even impossible, to change track in the middle of a process.

> **"** I believe that a major obstacle when it comes to new thinking is the silo mentality. If you have an organization that's built up of a lot of silos, people tend to work within their own silo. And then it's also difficult to feel any real affinity or loyalty with anyone or anything other than your own small group or department. You don't see the bigger picture or the problems or opportunities that actually affect everyone and impact the overall customer experience. I react quite immediately when I see signs of someone thinking, 'This is mine and that is yours.' That often takes a toll on customers or makes us less than adequate at solving problems and innovating. I think it's very important as a leader to show that we are *one* company, or *one* organization, that we're doing this together. That cooperation is a must.

Deloitte's *Global human capital trends* report (2018), based on survey responses from over 11,000 business leaders and HR managers in 124 countries, shows that the issue that most managers find most pressing right now is how to organize for the future. Only 14% of respondents believe that a traditional hierarchical structure allows their organization to perform effectively. An overwhelming majority (88%) believe that reorganization is important, but only 11% believe that they understand how they should go about it.

Today, there is a lot of talk about the importance of collaborating across organizational boundaries and knowledge barriers. One way to do this is to allow employees to form and dissolve their own cross-functional teams to steer themselves towards clear objectives. It becomes a way to organize around projects, not processes. *Here, we have problem/opportunity X. Which of us is best equipped to tackle it and can take it all the way to the end? Well, Anna from A, Samir from B, and Miriam and Bengt from C.* The team then has the mandate to take it from idea to realization, without first needing the approval of management or three different steering committees. The team also prefers to make several small, quick decisions in a trial-and- error process rather than a few large, "heavy," and potentially fatal decisions. In many organizations, an enormous amount of time is spent waiting for the green light from managers, for responses from colleagues, for deliverables from other players, for clearing up misunderstandings, for meetings and then more meetings. Hierarchies and structures frustrate and delay.

> ❚❚ I have worked abroad most of my life. In other countries, there's often a completely different hierarchy than what we are used to in Sweden. You don't question your boss or give your boss any feedback. Sometimes, the whole culture is based on the junior employees showing respect to the seniors. There can also be an outcry if you hop over someone in the hierarchy, even if you're a senior manager yourself. I remember once when I wanted to check something with a certain person and therefore went directly to him. I was then told that *I couldn't do that*, that I had to go through his boss first. Explain my case. Ask for permission. Coming from a Swedish context, you're not used to that kind of thing. It also becomes very inefficient. I don't think that an organization can achieve real, long-term success without a less pretentious internal cooperation. I usually encourage my employees not to think about hierarchies but to always talk directly to the person they need to talk to.

Cross-functional collaboration, both in teams and networks of teams, is a way of ticking off many wish-list items: increasing efficiency, executing faster, finding better solutions, getting better at solving complex problems, being more creative and innovative, and getting better at learning. This also strengthens internal cohesion. Interestingly, Deloitte's study shows that it's still relatively uncommon for an organization's most senior executives (C-level executives, i.e., those with titles beginning with "Chief," such as CEO, CFO, CIO, etc.) to collaborate on projects with other C-level executives. A whopping 73% of respondents said there was no such collaboration at the top of their organization. In short, it seems that there's a lot of talk about cross-functional teams, but when it comes down to it, the experts on the executive team are often experts in their own right, not experts at collaborating. Deloitte's analysts see this as a serious problem. They don't mince words, stating, "The message is clear: Senior managers need to get out of their silos and collaborate more with each other. To be able to navigate today's changing business environment and deal with challenges that affect multiple parts of the company, its senior leaders must *act as one*."

> As a new CEO, or new manager, you often inherit a team. There's nothing to say that everyone, or even anyone, should be replaced. There can be a lot of advantages to having people in the team who have been in the organization for a long time, provided there are also some who come in from outside and can look at things with fresh eyes. When the change is very extensive, it can be difficult if many on the team have strong roots in the old culture and old ways of working. Some are also the best at managing the status quo and incredibly good at their jobs, but just doing 'business as usual,' not driving change.
>
> But for me, the most important thing is that I feel I have the right people around me. I don't mean a certain *type* of person. If you have 14 people who all start competing all the time, it becomes a terrible team that no one wants to be part of! But everyone on the team has to be on the journey and really believe in what we're doing. And be prepared to fully cooperate with each other.

Diversity out there — uniformity in here

First of all, in a borderless world, it's bad to be "limited" internally. If there's movement out there, there must also be movement within. Now to the second part, to what this chapter is really about: if there's diversity out there, there cannot be uniformity within. And again, it has to start at the top.

Less than 15 years ago, there were more CEOs named Göran in Sweden's 500 largest companies than there were female CEOs. We chuckle at that today because it sounds like a joke. But Göran has merely retired.

"More Johans than women in CEO positions," wrote *Svenska Dagbladet* in February 2013. Then came Anders, and today the average CEO of a listed company is named Per. He is 54 years old and an economist or perhaps an engineer. In March 2018, *Dagens industri* reported that only 14% of large companies have a balanced (meaning gender-balanced) management team. In 2018, one in four CEOs on the Stock Exchange did not have a single woman on the management team.

> **"** I grew up in an environment where the message was that I could be whatever I wanted to be. The fact that I was a girl was not going to stop me, as there were no limitations related to gender. It was up to me to choose my path, and then if I worked hard, I would have the same opportunities as any man. But then I got into the working world. My first real job was at a bank in Geneva, and then I joined Ericsson in Lund in the mid-1990s. It took me a while to discover the power structures, but they were present in both places. There were no women in management positions, but not only that, there were no women being promoted, either. Not even if they worked extremely hard and delivered results. It was a pattern. I took this insight with me. As I've had roles later in life where I had the opportunity to change, I have always tried to do so. As soon as I entered a new role or management team, I addressed these issues. When I was recruiting people for the new management team at Telia, I was given a short list of potential candidates. I asked why there were only men on the list. I was told, 'We have looked but have not found any equally qualified women.' I said, 'Then you've been looking in the wrong places, because I know they exist,' and I gave the list back. It became a bit difficult and uncomfortable in the moment. I was in a hurry because I wanted to get the new management team in place quickly. But I had to stand firm. I said, 'Don't come back to me until half of that list is women.' And it worked. In all the leadership teams I've built during my career, there's been a

gender split of either 40/60, 60/40, or 50/50. And not because they've been chosen by gender — but because they've been chosen for their true competence and we searched in broader networks.

And something has certainly happened. There are more and more women sitting on boards and on management teams. There are more and more women in CEO positions in listed companies.

There is no doubt that progress is being made, albeit slowly.

The Allbright Foundation, which releases an annual report showing the state of gender equality in listed Swedish companies, believes that the change is an effect of Swedish companies adopting research that indicates that gender equality is good for business. It's also probably a consequence of the fact that more and more people, especially young people, think that diversity and gender equality issues are important and look for clear initiatives in this area among potential employers. Moreover, companies are being watched, especially the big ones. It doesn't look good to have a single woman on the board or in management, a "hostage" in the men's club.

But diversity is not just about gender. It's just as much about other things that can provide different perspectives on life, such as ethnicity, age, sexual orientation, gender identity or expression, religion or other beliefs, and disability. Today, almost 18% of Sweden's population was born in another country. Over 12,000 people live in same-sex marriages or registered partnerships. Half a million people in Sweden wear hearing aids, and 150,000 people use wheelchairs. The Catholic Church has over 100,000 members, and more than 300,000 people are members or active in a free church community, just to mention a few examples.

But even there, we stop too soon in our thinking. Few people think it's healthy to put together a group with only Görans, or only Annas or Ahmeds, for that matter. If we strive for diversity, we should not get stuck on the discriminatory aspects, on the most superficial, such as the fact that someone is from Iraq, is young and blonde, grew up in Biskopsgården, or is visually impaired. Diversity is not some kind of social duty or charity.

▌▌ For me, it's obvious that there should be equality and diversity, from the board and management all the way through the organization. This is partly because I've been the odd person out a few times myself. The tech industry is still very male-dominated, and I have often been the only woman in the group, the first woman in a certain position, or the only one who is not an engineer. Questioning and challenging norms can sometimes have an intrinsic value. But I see diversity as a strategic issue. Sometimes people say, 'We need diversity to meet the diversity of our customers.' But that feels old-fashioned. Maybe you used to have to talk about diversity in that way to get somewhere, but I think that's too narrow a perspective. I mean, if we want the best competence, we cannot at the same time exclude a large group of people just because they are women or have a different skin color or whatever. Nor do I think you can attract the right people if you don't take the issue of diversity seriously. If you attract strong women, for example, you will also attract strong men who understand that these issues are important.

But I believe that diversity is important for another reason. In my opinion, perhaps the most crucial reason in today's climate. If everyone thinks and feels the same way, it's almost impossible to drive change. I believe that the real power of diversity can be found when you stop focusing on what is the norm and what is different and start focusing on how people can come into their own and how we can create something new together.

If we are to have real diversity, then we must also have people from different sectors, as well as a diversity of skills, characteristics, abilities, motivations — everything that could conceivably contribute to thinking in different ways within the group, seeing different solutions to problems, seeing different needs, seeing different possibilities for how to work.

Then, it's also interesting that someone in the group is more focused on details and someone is more conceptual, that someone is more collaborative and someone is more competitive, that someone is more cautious and someone is more radical.

> ❚❚ I played a lot of soccer when I was young. I probably spent half my childhood on the soccer field, and when I got older, I coached girls' teams. I've brought that into the fundamentals of my leadership. I learned how important it is that the team works together. That doesn't mean that you want everyone to be the same. You can't win a game with 11 goalkeepers, no matter how great they are. The team is strong when everyone is allowed to play to their strengths, to do the thing they do the best. And when there's a good dynamic in the group, when you have the same purpose and goals and everyone is included in the team, then you can build something that's greater than the sum of its parts.

Life under the microscope

Some may object that it's difficult to know what is going on inside people, deep down. How do we really know if someone in the team is more introverted than extroverted, more flexible than structured, or more down-to-earth than head-in-the-clouds? What happens to the people on the tea when we have to collaborate with brand new team members or are under pressure for some reason? And what the heck do we do in the next step to ensure that everyone on the team gets to show up to work as their best selves?

> ❚❚ Today, there are plenty of proven tests and other tools that can help us get a clearer picture of that, although they may not give us the whole truth. There's also something of a revolution going on in the field of HR. Today's technology makes it possible to track, measure, and analyze not only customers but also employees. There's talk of an explosion of "people analytics." This is quite different from

measuring how many women are in management roles or how many absent days were recorded last year. This is about identifying patterns and adjusting processes to try to create the best possible conditions for employees to perform, collaborate, and solve problems. When are employees most effective? When do they learn the most, enjoy themselves the most, are the most creative, have the most fun? Why do they want to work here, and how do we take advantage of their talents? And if they choose to move on — *why*?

Of course, this development raises a lot of questions, like whether it's okay to track and monitor people so meticulously. But if we focus on the possibilities for the moment, we can perhaps look forward to a much more nuanced picture of the people who make up the organization, of their different personalities, motivations, strengths, and weaknesses, and of what engages and motivates each individual. Perhaps we'll also become much better at putting together teams that are capable of thinking in new ways and giving them the right conditions to succeed.

Birds of a feather

Of course, diversity is not always comfortable and pleasant. For example, research suggests a link between diversity and conflict in the workplace. Different experiences and opinions can clash, and communication can be difficult. But perhaps, in an innovative organization, we should see this friction as a positive thing?

▋▋ One thing I've learned to pay attention to is when everyone is extremely happy with their own team and their own manager. Then, I want to know more — do we truly have diversity in the team? Do they collaborate well with other teams? Do they take on challenges, and does the leader drive the necessary change? Cohesion in this sort of group can be very strong, and loyalty tends to be high. The employees give the manager top marks in all evaluations, and the manager gives the employees top marks in return: everyone is a star player. On the surface, such teams can be efficient, quick to make decisions, and super smooth to work in. But in my experience, teams that *really drive change, that want to constantly learn to include new and diverse talent, that challenge themselves in the face of transformation* are rarely consistently happy. In teams where diversity is actually expressed, not everything is always so smooth and comfortable.

Research shows that, in homogeneous groups, we're more likely to think alike and peer pressure is higher, which can make us less innovative and creative than we could be. An overly homogeneous group risks becoming an oxygen-deprived pool where no new ideas can emerge. In a world where innovation is key, it seems that birds of a feather may not flock so well together.

▮▮ I usually say that I'm more afraid of the questions that are *not* asked in the room than those that are. 'When you're bringing in someone new, it's so easy to think, 'Who do I know who knows this?' and look in your organization or among your friends and acquaintances and former colleagues. And then you sit there with your old buddies and think you're going to innovate!

I have to think, 'We don't need any more people like me in this team!' I think if you don't have people who come in with different experiences and see things differently, who come from different industries or countries, have different personalities, and are of different ages — a younger person might think thoughts that I would never think — then there are also a lot of questions that are never asked, that simply never come up. And then there's something going on

47

out there that you miss. In a world that moves at hyper speed, homogenous teams should be rated as a risk factor in any organization!

But we rode a Segway together!

So do we get an innovative team capable of driving change just because we have a great mix of skills, experience, opinions, personalities, and all that? No, hardly. We can't wrap it up in a bow quite yet.

Everyone has been part of a group that doesn't cooperate very well. Where everyone is overly polite and keen to be "one of the gang," or where there are conflicts over goals, tasks, roles, and values, and sub-groups and alliances are formed. Or where half are mostly silent. The group can be as diverse as you like, but it doesn't matter.

Sometimes someone senses that team members need to get to know each other better, so they try a dose of typical team building. You might divide into teams and compete with each other, play "prisoners at the conference," build a raft, ride a Segway, play paintball, or whatever. It's highly unlikely that the team functions better afterwards, despite the pleasant atmosphere and the many laughs. On the contrary, it may be the first day in a good long while with so little talk about important things, so little new thinking, or so much competition — not *cooperation*.

Most have also experienced the confusion that can arise when there's no clear vision, or at least a clear direction, for the work. What do we want to achieve? What are we striving for? It's easy to end up with 6, 8, or 12 people with different voices singing in a choir, but with different melodies.

But even if the goal is clear, and that big North Star — the higher purpose — lights up the road ahead, there is no guarantee that the team can actually drive change. Members must *communicate* with each other, they must truly listen to each other and be curious about new perspectives, they must talk to each other and interact with each other. Otherwise, diversity does not "work."

> **"** I'm not the kind of person who climbs mountains for seven days and then sees who can climb the furthest. I believe more in talking to each other for real about what's

important. And about what's difficult. And about who we are and what drives us forward. Otherwise, you can't move forward as a team. We can climb as many mountains as we like, or close our eyes and fall backwards and get caught as many times as we like, but we won't be a team if we can't say what's hard, ask for help, give each other support and feedback, say what we think. No one should be sitting there thinking, 'I might as well keep quiet because I don't know what *she* thinks about this or what *he* thinks....' I believe we can only truly work together when we share the same vision, when we passionately pursue the same goals, and when we can be straightforward and open with each other.

This leads us to the next chapter on the importance of a communicative culture and communicative leadership.

When Hélène takes over as CEO of Telia, the office is still located in Farsta. It's a large workspace, with over 3,000 employees. But her desk is at one end of the building. There's a quick side entrance, and a small staircase leads up to the office. In practice, she can come and go, even spend a whole day at work, without having to see anyone else out there. It's tasteful and secluded, perfect for thinking big thoughts and having important meetings in peace and quiet. "This isn't working," Hélène exclaims to one of her friends. "There is NO pulse here. Help me find a spot out there." Then, she sits among the others, her desk next to the Halebop team for almost a year, before moving to the new office in Solna.

* * *

On the floor of the small Telia store in Stockholm, Hélène stands awkwardly with a "New on the job" badge on her shirt. She is the company's CEO but can barely answer a single question from customers. She has to stand by and listen. Not only Hélène, but the entire management team is out working in different stores that day. They're having fun. It's not long before their pictures start to spread on Instagram and LinkedIn.

* * *

It's Friday. Hélène has taken a seat on the big wide staircase in the bistro at the head office in Solna. There's a palpable sense of space in the room, with many floors with high ceilings and many people moving around. The bistro is a hub. This is where employees and visitors come to grab a coffee, have lunch, and chat for a while. Hélène sits with her laptop on her lap and works, as she often does on Fridays. She doesn't look particularly CEO-like or busy or important, but more like anyone else. And she rarely sits alone for any length of time. Once in a while, someone comes up to her to exchange a few words. Sometimes, after just an hour or so, she's gained more valuable information about what's going on in the company than she might otherwise get in a whole day. This is what Hélène calls meeting-free Friday afternoons — no formal meetings, but a chance to cross paths with team members from different parts of the organization. And they all know where to find her on a Friday afternoon.

4

Ear to the ground

All organizations communicate. Marketing departments and PR agencies are buzzing with activity. Campaigns and new content are created for the website and social media, attractive launches of new products are arranged, films are made, customer magazines are produced, newsletters are sent out, advertising texts and press releases are written, events are arranged, conference materials and profile products are developed. And, of course, someone makes sure that the vision and values are visible on the website and on posters, coffee mugs, t-shirts, banners, and feather flags.

But not all organizations are communicative.

On the customer's terms

Today, there's a great opportunity to find out what customers actually want to do or know or buy, and then shape messaging and offerings accordingly. Every click on the website, every purchase in the store, every opened email, every swipe of the membership card, etc., can be linked to different registers and processed into insights about what the target group, down to each individual, wants and needs. But customers are also increasingly demanding. Karin Zingmark notes in *Maxa snacket* (2017) that they are less and less entertained by being "sold" something. They're increasingly opposed to any attempt to influence them without them asking for it. They prefer the authentic and unpolished. Better a recommendation from a friend than from a slick salesperson. Better a proud employee's spontaneous comment about their employer on Twitter, including a few typos, than the polished, proofread message produced by an agency. Zingmark notes that "the packaged message is blasé."

Customers are also less and less entertained by intrusive, *disruptive* communications. But they are plenty disturbed. By persistent telemarketers,

TV commercials, and unwanted newsletters. By ads in the middle of Facebook feeds and flickering billboards in town. By text messages reminding them to USE THE DISCOUNT CODE BEFORE IT'S TOO LATE. By push notifications that they can't be bothered to turn off. By chatty salespeople in the middle of the mall that they have to walk around to avoid accidentally buying something from (or punching in the face).

> **"** At EMC, Philippe and I talked about how what we really needed to do was move towards something like an old-fashioned country store — but with a digital twist. The person behind the counter in the country store often knew each customer personally and knew what that particular customer wanted and needed. Technology has allowed us to get close to our customers in a whole new way. But they also expect more from us, they expect more from our communication. In the past, you could perhaps push out your messaging and campaigns and products and keep your fingers crossed that customers would like them. Or try to shout the loudest so that you cut through the noise. But that doesn't work anymore. Soon, no company will be able to get away with 'talking up' its own great offers without first checking what each individual customer wants, wants to see, wants to know, or wants to do.

When everything and everyone communicates

Customers are not only demanding more — they're demanding it more loudly than ever. Technology has handed them a megaphone. Today, they are constantly connected and always ready to comment, rate, praise, or dismiss. It's like a spotlight that can be shone on the organization at any time. Even on its darker corners: "I think your commercial is sexist. What were you thinking there?"; "I applied for a job with you but then never got a 'no thanks' message, just silence. Bad!"; "It says on your website that you work with diversity, so why are there only middle-aged men in management?" If the posts are impactful or accurate enough, or if they are responded to in a clumsy way, they spread like wildfire, read by tens of thousands or even more. And once that fire starts, it doesn't matter what the website says, what the chairperson tells journalists, or how good the commercial is.

> Today, each individual customer has more power over the brand than before. And so does every single employee. This also means that *everything* we do as a company matters. From how we deal with a single irritated customer on Twitter to the demands we make on our subcontractors to the people we recruit to the management team. Or how we manage the recruitment process and take care of our employees in the here and now. Everyone and everything communicate. Every decision made, every collaboration, every day-to-day action. Even what we choose *not* to do. No CEO or marketing department has control over the company's image anymore. That control is shared by customers, employees, and everyone else who comes into contact with the company. I believe that we must dare to recognize this, and also dare to let go of a little control. We need to take steps towards decentralizing the responsibility for internal communication. I believe in a more spontaneous, personal, and responsive communication that we all manage together. If it's old-fashioned to think that you can only 'talk the talk,' then it's equally old-fashioned to think that only a few people should do the talking.

Communication for innovation

With everyone and everything communicating, and with a megaphone in hand, you have to be very sleepy not to feel a certain amount of pressure. There's so much you can do! So much to learn, so much to improve, so much to check and measure and compare! It's easy to get caught up in all the musts. "We must be more active in...", "We must get better at...", "We must learn to analyze..." The fear of falling hopelessly behind, of not doing enough, can act as fuel for a while. But in order not to succumb to the workload, you need a more enjoyable and meaningful answer to the "why" question than "because we must." Something that generates energy and that gathers and focuses that energy in the right direction.

> **❚❚** I come from a marketing background, so for me what's happening now is extremely exciting. It's become much easier to measure the real effects of different communication efforts: Are you spending time and money on the right things? Now, there are also lots of new channels and new opportunities to tell you what you as a company can help with and what you as a leader stand for. I don't go around thinking that I should post something on Instagram because I *must*. I do it because I *want to*. And technology gives us new opportunities to find out what customers really like and don't like. If we start with customer obsession, it becomes quite straightforward. Because then it becomes, first and foremost, a question of listening. Customers, especially dissatisfied ones, can help us find answers to perhaps the most important question of all: *What should we do differently? What can we do better?*

And maybe that's where we have it, a purpose worthy of the name. Communication for improvement, or perhaps even *communication for innovation*. With that in mind, it's time to stop "talking at" and actually start listening. And then the responsibility for putting your ear to the ground cannot rest on just a few people at the top or on some overburdened communications officers in the marketing department. It's not about producing an even better-looking commercial, but about creating an organization that is responsive, curious, open, and collaborative at a strategic level, and across all its operations.

The ideas that come from outside

So what could "communication for innovation" mean in practice? We can see that it's partly about an outside-in perspective, i.e., where outside thoughts, opinions, and ideas are allowed to flow into the organization and influence its innovation processes. Keeping an "ear to the ground" when the ground is outside the building. This kind of organization actively listens to customers in order to improve its own products (services, offerings, etc.). It's not only a world champion in collecting and analyzing data on customer and potential customer behavior, but also in encouraging all employees who interact with customers in their daily work to listen to what customers think and feel, what frustrates them, what they ask for, and what they want more of. It also ensures that employees who don't normally meet customers are actually out in the real world doing just that. And again, this has to start at the top, like with the CEO or preferably the entire management team out and about "practicing" in their own organization.

In a large organization, there may be many employees who don't naturally come into contact with customers on a daily basis. Then, you may need to help with that.

> ❚❚ In all offices, in elevators and corridors and wherever people move around, we installed screens where the Twitter feed was running. Everyone could see in real time what customers, employees, and others were saying about Telia. It was a way to get closer to customers, but also to keep us on our toes. In front of those screens, myself, our chairperson, or anyone else could stand right alongside customers or journalists or whomever. If one of our customers has a problem or dissatisfaction with something, it suddenly affects everyone, the whole company, the whole brand. It becomes somehow personal. And it truly shows that we care — and that we want transparency even when it hurts.

A communicative organization also has open borders in a broader sense, in the sense of integrating customers, suppliers, public agencies, universities, start-up companies, perhaps even competitors, in the development of new products and services and in various aspects of the organization's development.

> ❚❚ I believe that transparency is an important part of this, to dare to be open with figures and strategies and with what's going on. And dare to invite new things. Maybe test

open innovation and crowdsourcing in some part of the business. Not to think that we have all the skills we need within our own walls. I only have to look to myself: I often bring in outside help when I don't have the right skills on my own. Or ask those who are completely new to the organization what they see. You can get a lot of input by listening to people who look at the business from the outside. I generally believe in broad cooperation with people who may have different perspectives and see different solutions to problems. I think you should strive for diversity here, too.

The ideas that come from within

Not all good ideas come from outside. In many cases, your own employees know very well what could be improved and may also have ideas about how to create something completely new. There used to be a belief that only a few exceptionally creative and fearless individuals were capable of radical innovation and turning ideas into reality. But the myth of the lone genius, who sits in their room and invents something that changes the world, seems to have passed its sell-by date. In *The Silicon Valley model,* Annika Steiber and Sverker Alänge note that Google, Tesla, and other continuously innovating companies are characterized by a deeply rooted belief that human beings, each individual in the company, want and need to be creative — and will be when in the right environment.

Since we're focusing on communication here, the question becomes: How can we communicate with each other internally in a way that helps foster that environment? One that contributes to creativity and new thoughts and ideas?

If the first one was an "outside-in" perspective, we can call this second one an "inside-out" perspective. Here, it's perhaps not so much about no longer "talking at," but more about no longer silencing. Or at least ensuring that employees are both willing and able to express their thoughts and ideas. An "ear to the ground," when the ground is the very floor under the employees' feet.

In the previous chapter, covering diversity and collaboration, we noted towards the end that a diverse team doesn't automatically drive change and generate new values. It's not enough for us to have a quantitatively equal organization or superficially heterogeneous teams.

For diversity to "work," team members must actually communicate with each other. They must be willing to listen to each other — including colleagues with different perspectives and opinions — and they must be willing to express themselves even when they don't think and feel the same way as others in the group. They need to be able to raise difficult issues, give each other feedback, and question each other's truths.

> In Sweden, we have a leg up. We're already collaboration-oriented, and we tend to be good at team sports and have comparatively flat organizations. But we sometimes confuse *collaboration* with *consensus*. For me, successful collaboration is not when everyone agrees and has the same views. Collaboration happens when people genuinely express their differences, and the group members listen and build on each other's ideas and make the group stronger. If you have a culture of consensus, there's a risk that those with different ideas and opinions choose to keep quiet about them just to get the group to agree. And then, we are there again, missing a lot of things. I think it's important that I as a leader show in different ways that it's okay to stand out, that I look for that different question, that different perspective. That thinking differently is something I like and want to see more of.

This brings us to something that ties together diversity, communication, and innovation: *inclusion*. Inclusive communication can be about the words we choose when sending an invitation to the staff party and about how the website or the physical office environment is designed. Someone who's in a same-sex relationship, speaks Swedish with less fluency, is older or younger than everyone else, or in some other way deviates from the norm should not feel "wrong," invisible, unwelcome, or excluded. The price for that is too high – for both the individual and the organization.

But inclusion is more than that. It's about dropping the veil of consensus and working together.

In an employee-obsessed organization with its ear to the ground, you work actively to build trust and confidence in each team through exercises that help to increase psychological safety and respect among team members. You may need to enlist the help of a skilled consultant or two to get a little closer and to have a chance to practice giving and receiving feedback. Maybe you need to think about how you communicate with each other at work. Maybe you need help to practice inclusive leadership — across your organization.

Cecilia Duberg notes in *Elefanteffekten* (2018) that most of us may need to develop our listening skills. We're often very interested in expressing our own opinions and points of view, but really it's just ruminating on what we already know and can do. We fight, more or less vehemently, to maintain the worldview we already have. We fight for control. Something as simple as no longer responding to others' comments with the little word "but" ("Sure, but…", "I know, but…") can have a big impact. Less fighting and more listening. Because the point was not "communication for control," but the opposite — communication for innovation. Sometimes internal structures, hierarchies, and approaches to work can get in the way of listening and communicating internally and ultimately hinder progress. There may be a need for a broader range of interfaces between employees and between teams or a broader range of forums for testing out and getting feedback on new ideas. Perhaps the meter-thick walls between rooms in the impressive fortress give the impression that people are much farther away from each other than they really are.

> **❚❚** We had a big corporate group meeting with over 100 managers to talk about why the change wasn't going faster. What was standing in the way? We worked all morning to identify the obstacles and wrote them down on sticky notes. While everyone was having lunch, the room was rearranged to have a circle of chairs in the middle where the management sat, and then more circles outside of that for the next level of managers, and then the next.

Lisa Lindström, CEO of Doberman, who organized the meeting, said, 'Now, you have identified the barriers. You who are in this room, you're the ones who can tear them down.' In that inner circle, there were two empty chairs. Anyone who wanted could go in there, take a seat and have their say. It was a transparent meeting. And as Lisa said, why not permanently have an open, rotating seat among top management?

Communicative leadership

If you as a CEO want your employees to express themselves, to be responsive, present, open, and communicative — well, you have to start with yourself.

❚❚ In the past, managers could sit in a glass office at the top of the building and send out a message to their employees once a month. That doesn't work anymore. You have to dare to show yourself, dare to respond to negative feedback. If I were to give any advice, it would be: Be present and involved, skip PowerPoints, listen, and ask questions! Travel around, visit different customers, partners, and shops and different parts of the business. It gives you a lot of information and provokes a lot of thoughts. And encourage the organization to challenge you — for example, through reverse mentoring or by participating in various groups where you share what you're sure of and unsure of and ask for input. Invite new people into your meetings who will offer new and unexpected perspectives. When it comes to social media, I would also never dream of letting someone else manage my Twitter or LinkedIn account or write what I should say when I'm out and about. That would be far too artificial because the value lies not in the fact that what I write is so perfect, but in the fact that it's my personal voice. I wouldn't let someone else sit and answer emails or questions that were addressed directly to me, because then there's a big risk that I'll get a slightly tweaked version of reality. And I like to sit for at least a few hours every week in a place where many people move around, where I'm visible, where the step of coming up to me and saying or asking something becomes easier to take.

D on't you know how Twitter works?!" The communications officer's stressed voice on the phone. Hélène has recently taken over as CEO of Telia Sweden, but it's still summer, and she's now on vacation — as is a large part of the organization. For a few days, she's been keeping an eye on what's being said on Twitter about the company to get a sense of what's going on out there. What do customers think? What are they annoyed about? What do they like? One morning, she discovers a recent comment from a customer in distress. It's something about the technology, something that should work but doesn't, and it affects the customer's children who are home alone. Hélène is convinced that the comment will be answered very soon. Someone will see it shortly and make sure that the customer gets help.

But nothing happens. And so the hours pass.

These summer days, Hélène has been thinking a lot about the future of Telia. And about her own role as CEO. A little "soul searching" to try to identify what's needed to bring the company into the future. In 2015, Telia is a somewhat disjointed organization. When the Swedish state sold off Telia in the summer of 2000, almost a million Swedes took up that offer and bought Telia shares. But then it sank like a stone, and that was the beginning of a long trek back on the stock market. The newspapers wrote about "the stock market failure of the century" and how "the Swedes have been cheated." Then came the Eurasia story. According to the indictment, in 2007-2010, Telia Sonera bribed the dictator's daughter Gulnara Karimova with SEK 3 billion to operate in Uzbekistan. At home, competitors have also emerged, sometimes offering customers cheaper and better services and sometimes giving them better treatment.

And now there is still no response to the comment on Twitter.

Telia needs a fresh start.

Finally, Hélène picks up the phone and answers the customer's comment herself. She also adds her own private telephone number and writes that the customer can contact her directly and that she will see what she can do. She does this to get feedback from the customer. She also does it to show the organization that something needs to change, and in what direction. Technical problems are already the worst, but add bad service as well and people lose their minds. *Customer focus*, Hélène realizes, is too weak a phrase for what's required here. *Customer obsession* is better. And it has to start at the top, with herself, with what she says and does.

Then, the phone rings. It's not the customer, but the communications department. Doesn't Hélène know that everyone can now see her private number?! Doesn't she know how Twitter works?

"Yes," says Hélène, "I know how Twitter works."

5

The power of storytelling

Storytelling is now used in many organizations to strengthen their brand. In short, it involves using stories to show what you stand for and what you can offer, in a way that evokes emotions and inspires commitment from customers, partners, and other stakeholders. It's a way of "populating" the brand, giving it some flesh and blood — some soul. Many people who hear the word "storytelling" therefore instantly think of marketing and PR, of advertising messages that show how the company is saving the world a little bit. Or they associate the idea with funny commercials that are easy to relate to, where an ordinary person (the hero), with the help of the company's product/service, solves their problem, impresses their love, is a better parent, wins the race, and so on. A story of this kind can be a much more powerful way of reaching people than just trumpeting out "we think sustainability is important" or "we make cheap furniture," or "buy our shoes." By the way, IKEA is world famous for its storytelling. So are Airbnb, Google, and Nike.

However, this type of more outward-looking storytelling is not what this chapter is primarily concerned with. Rather, it's the storytelling that is directed inwards to the organization itself to show employees what the big flowery words actually mean. It's about consciously, continuously, and thoughtfully highlighting stories that aim to inspire and empower employees and show them what the change journey is about, where the organization is headed, and what kind of behavior is going to take the organization in that direction. Leaving them with an emotional "a-ha!" instead of a blank stare. This is not achieved with three points and a chart, but by conveying a feeling that inspires action. A good story is the antithesis of the dry PowerPoint presentation. This makes storytelling an unbeatable tool during a change journey.

▌▌ Leaders are often used to changes that involve, for example, cost savings and are thus more used to communicating about those topics. However, they are not as good at communicating the purpose, the aspirational story, and the culture — and thereby helping people understand the vision, what they want to achieve, and what's *meaningful* about it. For me, storytelling is about showing what you want to do and why. It's a way of asking, 'Do you want to be part of this journey?'

The house is on fire!

According to change guru John P. Kotter, more than half of all change initiatives fail because the challenges facing the organization are not taken seriously enough. In *Leading Change* (1996), and even more so in later books, Kotter emphasizes the importance of creating a "sense of urgency" for change to occur.

But this is easier said than done. Because it's not always easy to see — to *feel* — why it's important to change and why it's urgent. Especially if the company is making money and not in an obvious crisis — at least not yet.

❚❚ Perhaps the surveys show that customers are satisfied, and you compare yourself to the same old competitors in the industry and feel a little bad about not being at the forefront of technology. But then you forget to look at what's happening in other industries or forget to look at what customers value most. Like freedom of movement, for example. It's quite serious if you continue to tie customers up in long subscriptions when your competitors stop doing that. Or if you waste more of your customers' time than others do. Perhaps you're so focused on internal efficiency that you miss the fact that your own structures force customers to open another letter, make another choice, remember another password, make another call. After all, time is one of the most precious things we humans have. Today, we're not only competing with others in the same industry, but with the very best in every possible industry. For example, if it's really easy to pay through another provider, or find the right website, get technical support, or have something delivered to your door within 24 hours, why should customers tolerate inferior service from us?

I think an important task as a leader is not to focus on what the closest competitors are doing, but to keep an eye on what's happening in the broader world around your company and your customers, and then share what you see with your employees. I often deliberately bring up examples of areas for improvement during meetings, even large meetings where all staff can see and hear me. Such as the figures showing that young people choose competitors, or showing that you're indeed successful among a small target group where you've always been successful but are losing the newer high-growth target groups. Sometimes, it's actually quite urgent and important to move on or rethink.

Pride as a springboard

But there's a catch. Too great a sense of urgency gets heavy. Employees who are constantly told about everything that's not optimally working or that others are doing better will soon become discouraged. How do you point out the seriousness of the situation in a way that doesn't depress or paralyze, but rather increases the will to change?

In the book *Stolthet som strategi* (2018), Elin Alsiok and Caroline Stenbacka Nordström describe the importance of pride for employees' sense of responsibility, well-being, and motivation, for how employees are treated — and, from a broader perspective, for the success and future of the organization. Their advice: Focus on what's already good and already working and build on it.

Anyone who thinks that a sense of urgency alone will get the ball of change rolling may need to think again. In most organizations, there are lots of things that do not work optimally and that are more or less urgent and important to change. But hanging the communication of the change journey entirely on the message "You get that the house is on fire, right?!" is not necessarily the right way to go. It's quite possible to stress the hell out of people without anything happening at all. The energy and desire to contribute to a change can instead be found by focusing on all that the organization has done and is doing and on the meaning it carries for its customers and perhaps for society as a whole. For instance, by highlighting positive examples that reflect what the journey is all about, stories that are in line with the change you want to see. Matts Heijbel, an early Swedish advocate for storytelling, talks about "harvesting" your stories, in the sense of taking advantage of what's already there. Because there's definitely a lot going on in the day to day that's worth picking up and spreading around. You just have to keep your eyes and ears open.

> **"** Has anyone done anything out of the ordinary to help a customer in trouble? This is customer obsession in action. Have we contributed to solving a social problem? Then that story can show what we do when we're making the world a little better. Or have we, together with others, done something completely new and revolutionary? Such as when Telia contributed to Sweden becoming the first country in the world to remotely operate air traffic control towers. Or take the Boliden example, where a large-scale collaboration among many operators made it possible to remotely operate driverless mining vehicles and use mobile phones 400 meters into the mountain. This is incredibly exciting!
>
> If you combine the ingredients, i.e., make your employees feel both a sense of urgency *and* pride, you can have an organization with both the desire to be part of the journey and the drive that comes from realizing the urgency. I want people to feel proud because there's enormous power in pride. Just not proud and *satisfied*. Because then it's like what happened to Nokia.

Storytelling is a strategic tool that, when used correctly, can strengthen the culture while also creating brand awareness and attracting people who consider what the organization does and stands for to be important. It can be an engaging way to communicate the change journey not only with employees but with the outside world.

> **"** What's to say that investors and analysts don't need anything beyond the charts, tables, and figures of quarterly reports? Why not tell them, 'We're going to embark on this journey, and it'll take three years, but you'll see a completely new organization after those three years, and that will show up in X, Y, and Z.' Sure, you may need to highlight different stories for different audiences, and sometimes translate the message into numbers, but we're all human after all. We just want to understand what's happening and where we're going — and we want to be part of that journey.

Patrik Widlund explains in his book *Digital transformation* (2018) that Amazon asked investors to be patient with dividends because all the money was needed to reinvest in development. He notes that the shareholders who thought it was a good idea are fortunate today. What was once an online bookstore is now the world's largest e-commerce platform.

Storydoing — bringing the story to life

We've discussed in several chapters the importance of leaders practicing what they preach, and here we are again. Few things say as much about where an organization is headed than what its leaders actually *do*.

If you truly believe in *diversity*, few things are as powerful as sending back a list of all-male candidates for a managerial role: "Don't come back to me until that list is half women." That sort of thing spreads quickly in the organization. "Did you hear that she…?" If you truly believe in having your *ear to the ground*, then you must venture out of your fancy office and meet employees and customers, work in the store, sit on the stairs in the bistro, go out digging to install fiber, listen to customer service calls, and write your own social media posts, including a few too many enthusiastic exclamation points and the occasional typo. If you truly believe in *customer obsession,* that message can scarcely be communicated more effectively than by posting your private phone number on Twitter so that an angry customer is not met with silence. Or by creating a new role directly under the CEO — Head of Customer Experience — to show that customer obsession is a top priority. If you truly believe in *employee obsession*, then you can't miss an opportunity to encourage and reward those who contribute to forward movement.

> How do you get a whole organization to change? How do you activate so many people? How do you prove that the change you're talking about is what you really stand for? Traditionally, you broadcast that change through PowerPoints. I don't believe in that. It's not enough, especially in a large, established organization with a strong immune system. I believe in *doing.* As a leader all the time, every single day, demonstrate through action the direction you want the organization to move. I think this is how you can move from a two-dimensional leadership approach to a three-dimensional one.

If storytelling is communicating through stories, then "storydoing" is the very essence of that. It's fundamentally about authenticity, about standing by what you say and showing with your actions what you want to achieve and strive for — *living the* story.

Talk the walk

In his book *Simply brilliant* (2016), William C. Taylor shows illustrates through a variety of examples from both well-known and unknown companies that leaders who think outside the box in terms of what it takes to succeed also tend to communicate in a slightly different way. For example, by deliberately using stories to get their message across. Or by being more personal in the way they communicate and using different words than those encountered in old standard business vocabulary. Or by demonstrating through their own behavior what kind of change they want to see, but also talking a lot about why they do what they do.

> **▌▌** Walking the talk is not always enough. You may also need to talk about what you do over and over again and in tons of different ways, both to your employees and to the outside world, to quite simply "talk the walk."

I've told that Twitter story many times because it illustrates what I mean by customer obsession. It makes it easier to understand what I'm saying.

The never-ending story

If hardly a day goes by without you as a leader standing in front of people and talking about the change journey — and if you constantly "walk the talk" *and* "talk the walk" — it's easy to think that you've almost finished communicating. Especially if you're a bit impatient as a person. You may have stood on stage time and again and talked about the challenge and the path and the purpose and the values, tweeted like crazy, traveled around the country to visit all the offices, connected with customer service, sat on countless panels and in interview chairs. Perhaps you've been so visible, communicative, and outgoing as a leader that employees are starting to refer to you as "our Foreign Minister." Surely the message must have gotten through? Surely everyone already understands what the journey is about, what you want to achieve and why?

Odell notes in *Förändringshandboken* that one of the most common mistakes organizations make is to under-communicate. He argues that it's not enough to repeat a message of change 8 or 12 times, or only via a few channels. He recommends repeating it at least 25 times. To *drive it home*. On social media, on the intranet, in meetings large and small, in newsletters, in interviews and panel discussions, on notice boards and in every other conceivable way.

And this is where stories, which can be endlessly varied, come to the rescue. A leader can only say the phrase "customer obsessed" so many times before employees start rolling their eyes.

Being told yet again that "customer focus is important" is one thing, but hearing that a colleague has been named "Customer-Obsessed Employee of the Year" is another. What has that person done to deserve that award? Or being told that, in order to bother as few customers as possible, the company chose to cover the cost of updating the system in the middle of the night instead of in the middle of the live Eurovision broadcast. It's one thing to see yet another slide with the "We are digitizaling Sweden" headline, but another to read in the newspaper that the company has just launched a new nationwide network for connected gadgets or that the entire countryside around Kalmar is now getting fiber. It's one thing to say somewhere on the website that you want to contribute to a better society, but it's quite another to hear that the company is supporting a project where young people teach retirees to become more digital, or that patients can now securely connect via an app or computer to get in touch with healthcare professionals from their local hospital.

Storytelling, in a nutshell, because it's just so much more fun that way!

B ecause I'm happy — clap along — if you feel — like a room without a roof...!" On the large staircase in the middle of the bistro on the 7th floor, in front of surprised employees, Telia Sweden's entire management team is singing at the top of their lungs. It's the Pharrell Williams song "Happy," and they've spent half the day practicing. There had never been any plans to go out and sing in front of the staff. It was a whim. Hélène had suddenly exclaimed, "Let's go out and sing for the others!" The group left the safe conference room with a slightly elevated pulse. This had all started six months earlier. Hélène had sat on a stage with the artist and musical instructor Eva Hillered to talk about the link between music, creativity, and leadership. The moderator was Lisa Lindström, CEO of the digital design agency Doberman. The meeting had sparked an idea. Could Telia Sweden's management team come together for a day of singing? Or to take it a step further, in this age of digitalization, could they try the theme "Singing & Coding"? Some of the management team were engineers at heart, but no one was a brilliant coder. No one was a star at singing, for that matter. In other words, the conditions were excellent. It was decided, then — the management team was invited to an all-day workshop for singing and coding. They weren't given a detailed description of what would happen. Hélène didn't know what was going to happen, either, and she prayed that the day wouldn't end in failure.

One of the participants showed up, took a few steps into the room, saw the keyboard that Lisa Lindström and Eva Hillered had brought with them, and muttered, "Oh my God." He had googled "Singing & Coding" but found nothing at all. He thought it might be some hot new management technique, and deep down, he was hoping that the "Singing" part was about anything but actual singing.

But they were meant to sing. Half the day was spent sitting at computers and coding, and the other half was spent standing in a semi-circle and singing. Tentatively at first, then with increasing confidence. Finally, they sounded almost like a choir. Almost.

And now here they suddenly are standing in the bistro in front of the astonished employees, swaying to the music and clapping to the beat. They aren't exactly songbirds, but they sing anyway, tapping their toes.

Lisa scans the crowd of spectators in the bistro and sees something in their eyes. They seem to understand that nobody on the management team feels completely comfortable standing there singing. They seem to realize that nobody finds this easy. Some of the spectators look simultaneously skeptical and amused. Or possibly embarrassed. Others crack a smile. Some, in their surprise, forget to close their mouths.

And then they start tweeting.

6

The fearless organization

In recent years, interest in agile working methods has increased. This is not surprising. Many people are already familiar with lean and the ideas about flow, efficiency, and teamwork, about streamlining processes so that everything that doesn't contribute to creating value is removed. There are many connections between lean and agile ideas and methods. Originally, sometime in the 1990s, agile was associated with software development, in projects where it was clearly inefficient to stay in one room and try to come up with the Ultimate Solution (and spend half the time on paperwork). Where the end goal was undefined. Where it was necessary to involve the customer or client early and then continuously deliver, check, adjust, improve, and take the next step in rapid cycles.

The circumstances that applied in some IT projects back then can now apply in many more contexts. Remember that roaring alpine stream in the fog? How the water rises and uncertainty grows? Standing there on the beach, you quickly realize that your heavy backpack poses a problem. You can't wobble on slippery rocks with a huge backpack full of stuff. You'lll have to empty it of anything that isn't absolutely necessary, even if there are risks involved and even if it feels generally crummy — hey, that stuff wasn't free!

Just as quickly, you realize that it's necessary to step out without knowing whether the path you've chosen is the right one. Once on the first rock, you have to reassess the situation. You may discover a new opportunity from your new position or realize how you can improve your technique to increase your chances of getting across.

For many businesses today, the terrain is unknown, the end goal subject to change or difficult to define in advance, and the unpredictability and complexity high. Not to mention that cutthroat competition — and as I said, there's a lot of urgency. Nobody can afford to spend a lot of time and effort creating something that customers don't want.

It's true that few people claim that agile methods are the solution to everything. But the agile philosophy is appealing. One reason is its focus on people and collaboration, feedback, and communication. If agile methods used to be the most talked about, now it's "agile organizations" and "agile leadership." More and more people are realizing that you don't become agile just by applying a little agile varnish here and there. Soon, we may not hear as many comments like, "Yes, we work in an agile way. We use scrum, and so on."

But this chapter hasn't been titled *Quick feet and quick minds* or *Most agile wins*. It's not about how to introduce an agile approach on a broad front. Because if agile methods and approaches are a cure-all (or one cure of many), what is the real problem? All those steering committees, management levels, and closed rooms, all the budgets, Excel spreadsheets, and numerous KPIs, all the methods and processes and procedures, all the instructions, requirements specifications, and PowerPoint presentations — what are they symptoms of? And why on earth are we clinging to structure and ways of working that were created for a different time with a very different set of conditions?

Belts and suspenders

Let us return for a moment to our alpine stream and imagine that we're still standing there on the bank. There are three things that would make us maximally stagnant. Individually, or in a deadly mixture:

We cannot.

We don't want to.

We don't dare.

We cannot because we lack the right conditions, such as the proper skills, resources, or tools. Or because there are structures that inhibit us, such as old hierarchies and systems of governance and control. Or because we draw too sharp a line between *my* responsibility and *my* goals and *your* responsibility and *your* goals. Having teams that are too homogeneous, non-functioning, and non-inclusive is also part of it. As is being bad at listening, at learning, and at taking advantage of the lessons we learn along the way.

We don't want to because we don't see the point. We don't have an inspiring answer to the "why" question, we don't understand where we're going and why our actions matter. We are unmotivated and disengaged, and we are not having fun.

We don't dare because we're afraid of the consequences of trying and failing.

The first two points have been addressed in previous chapters. Now for the third. If we remain on the beach paralyzed by fear, we will get absolutely nowhere. We must have the courage to act despite the uncertain circumstances. Fear also hampers every step, even if we dare to take that first step. Should we anxiously hesitate on every stone, our progress will be hopelessly slow.

Being agile means moving smoothly and efficiently. By simplifying and eliminating anything superfluous, shortening lead times, promoting communication at all levels, and working closely with customers/clients and in rapid cycles or feedback loops, we're likely to become more agile. We solve problems faster. We become better at responding to customers' needs and wishes. We may also become more creative.

But are we getting bolder?

What if we turn the spotlight away from efficiency and agility and shine it instead on action?

Being willing and able is fundamental to action. Then, it's also necessary to examine the final piece of the puzzle. How can we create an organization that dares? That is, an organization where employees willingly rethink things in the middle of an ongoing process. Where they question and express their point of view even when it differs from the majority. Where they take initiative even when it's not expected, where they are open to both giving and receiving feedback, where they share and invite instead of closing the door and holding on to their own. Where they dare to be themselves. Where they take the plunge even if there's a risk of failure.

How do we create a fearless organization?

Self-esteem and self-confidence

We can start with the low-hanging fruit. We do not create a fearless organization through "management by fear," public scolding, and abrupt dismissals. Nor through an army of middle managers closely guarding their respective territories. Or through a culture of silence.

But let's explore the question a bit further. If digitalization — combined with everything else going on in the world right now — creates uncertainty in itself, then what would it take to prevent that feeling from becoming even more acute?

A sense of competence

To avoid getting stuck in a rut, we need to feel that we're up to the challenge. Having the right skills is key, of course. But *feeling competent* is just as important.

▌▌ When I took over as CEO of Telia, some of the old pride in the organization was gone. If we go back in time, there had been pride in the technology and the accessibility and world-class quality of the services. That self-image had been shattered by bribery scandals and other setbacks. Now, there were also competitors who were both quick-footed and innovative. In comparison, Telia could be seen as old-fashioned and slow-moving: a 'has-been.' A process of change had begun, but it needed to be both faster and deeper, and there were lots of things we needed to address. It would have been easy to go in with a message like 'Now we're leaving something bad behind us,' just to try to draw a line between the past and present. But that would not have been good. For me, it was obvious to highlight Telia's history and everything that the campus in Farsta stood for, the fantastic competence contained in the company, and everything there was to be proud of. It was from that platform that we would now take the next step. I think you need to feel some kind of solid ground under your feet if you're going to embark on a journey of change like this one. In fact, I think it's almost impossible to succeed with a really big change in an organization that isn't proud and secure. The feeling of competence can be strengthened not only by the experience of having done something good in the *past* but of doing something good *right now*, of succeeding in what we do. This feeling is reinforced when we can show what we're capable of and feel effective in our interactions with others. It can be strengthened further by recognizing all markers of progress, even small ones. Deci and Ryan, the two motivation researchers, have discovered something interesting in this regard: Many external rewards (money, good grades, nice perks, etc.) actually reduce your own inner drive. With one exception. The single form of external reward that increases intrinsic motivation? *Positive feedback*. Everyone knows by now that it's valuable (and generally nice) to celebrate successes, even small ones, but perhaps not *how* important it actually is.

A sense of competence can also be reinforced by the feeling that we're developing, learning something new, and becoming even better. The feeling of personal or professional growth is so pleasant that we want to relive it. We want to learn even more, to develop further. And we don't have to take giant steps to experience that feeling.

American researcher Theresa Amabile of the Harvard Business School describes in her book *The progress principle* (2011) how we get roughly the same thrill from small, sometimes even tiny, improvements and progress along the way as we do from reaching the end goal itself. This is good news for anyone who recognizes that "learning the most" trumps "knowing the most." By encouraging learning at all levels, we can kill two birds with one stone: we can strengthen the organization's capacity to act while at the same time taking steps towards a culture of learning and growth. A sense of competence can also be enhanced when we're given an opportunity to do something that feels a little unfamiliar and uncomfortable. There's research that shows that the part of the frontal lobe that's active when we learn something new switches off when there's no element of unpredictability in the situation. Without uncertainty, there's no learning.

❚❚ If I succeed in what I am already very good at, that has its value, and my self-confidence may grow a bit. But when I dare to take a risk, to do something I'm not used to or not comfortable with, and I 'survive,' then it has a different value. And here I believe a lot in showing that you do things outside your own comfort zone, in showing your own vulnerability as a leader.

Our sense of competence also gets a boost when we feel that we're allowed to fail. This is where a familiar question comes in — "What's the worst that can happen?" If the worst that can happen is losing your job, being publicly scolded, or being met with silence, then "the worst" is pretty awful. But if it's your boss and colleagues saying, "That's too bad, but better luck next time," then the risk is different. Not to mention if even unsuccessful efforts are recognized and "celebrated" as necessary steps in learning on the path forward.

> **▐▐** If you're serious as a leader about wanting people to dare to try, you need to show it. Reward and encourage that behavior. Promote people who have dared and who have broken new ground. That sends clear signals. And if it went wrong and cost money or whatever, then you can talk about it. Then, you might learn something for next time. Never punish genuine attempts to think and innovate.

A sense of belonging

To take this step, we need to feel equipped for the challenge, to feel "we got this." But that's not enough. An organization where someone on each team sits with the uncomfortable feeling of being "wrong" or stays silent even when they would rather or should object, contribute, or raise a question is an organization in trouble. For us to be willing and able to be ourselves and become the best version of ourselves, we need to be encouraged to express who we are.

Thoughts, opinions, feelings, experiences, motivations — the whole package.

> **▐▐** This is one of the reasons we need to put diversity and inclusion high up on the agenda. We cannot be satisfied with 'accepting' differences- They must be valued in

practice. They must be encouraged. I think it's very difficult to perform at your best if you feel that you can't really be yourself. You can't have a soccer team where one of the midfielders feels 'tolerated' or where two people on the team don't really feel like part of the community. No organization can afford to have employees who sit there holding themselves back a bit in their day-to-day work.

Of course, creating a culture where everyone feels they can truly show up and be their best selves is no easy task. But you can strive towards it. And you have to start somewhere.

❚❚ I believe that if you as a leader actively address an issue you're passionate about, such as gender equality, and your actions show that you think it's important, then you can get something started. Then, it won't be such a big leap to start thinking about diversity and inclusion in more areas. And for me, as I've said, inclusion is very much about communication, about having a culture where you can be open and honest with each other, where feedback is not the same as an annual performance review. Even with that, you have to start somewhere. For example, most of us aren't as used to giving each other feedback in everyday life. I think we may need to train ourselves a little there.

Perhaps what it comes down to is that we need to feel safe in the teams we're part of. Otherwise, there's a great risk that we are not truly ourselves and therefore cannot feel that unbridled sense of desire and energy and courage to step outside of the familiar and comfortable. A few years ago, when Google examined how their teams were performing, they discovered that the highest-performing teams were characterized by what they call "psychological safety." The massive two-year study showed that it was far more important for team members to feel safe in the group than for the team to have a perfect mix of skills and personalities. In a psychologically safe team, people feel that they can speak their minds, come up with ideas, and stick their necks out without the risk of being punished.

They feel that they can be part of the team even if they make mistakes, that no one will laugh at their ideas, and that everyone wants to move forward together.

In order for us to be willing and able to be ourselves, we also need to be listened to and taken seriously, whether in a meeting room or a break room. That could look like not being waved away or labeled as backwards when we express (perhaps fully justified) anger or concern about some aspect of the change process. Or not feeling encouraged to come up with ideas if they just get blocked and tucked away in some dark corner. Finally, we need to be shown actual appreciation. In words and in actions.

A sense of being trusted

In some organizations, silo structures and hierarchies are so pervasive that they become barriers to employee efficiency and the company's success. Those who have power protect it, and those without power do nothing without the approval of a superior. If there's a deeply rooted tradition of pointing out the direction — this way, that way, up, or down — nobody who encounters a problem outside their area will imagine taking responsibility for solving it themselves. Such an organization moves forward much more slowly, if at all, than one with a culture of trust in the common sense and decision-making of its people.

> My starting assumption is that people can be trusted. And I think you should strive to create a culture of consistent trust. You can do this in all sorts of ways. It can be about having free working hours or letting people sit and work in a café in the city if they want to. It can be about giving teams a mandate to act on their own judgment, to ensure that those closest to a problem can solve it in the way they think is best. I believe that more teams need to be able to choose their way of working, agile or not, without any interference from a manager.

Then, I think it's very counterproductive if I as a leader always come up with ready-made answers, as if I myself always know what's best. It's much better to ask questions, genuinely listen, and seek feedback and advice. Encouraging self- leadership is basically about showing trust, about believing that every person can actually take responsibility for themselves. Not so long ago, I was asked, 'What do you think leaders need to show less of?' My immediate answer was *distrust*.

Fearless leadership

Many of the points above are fundamentally about leadership, the approach and priorities of management and the board. It must start at the top to become real and successfully reach all the way through the organization.

So what kind of leader do we want in our fearless organization? Daniel Goleman, the man behind the concept of emotional intelligence or EQ, is considered one of the greats in the field of change management because his perspective differs from — or complements — the more "step-by-step" perspective of Kotter and others. Goleman's study of nearly 200 international companies showed that managers with emotional intelligence are more effective as leaders. Goal orientation and intelligence (IQ) were not enough to succeed. Other softer qualities were also needed.

According to Goleman, leaders with high EQ have five typical characteristics (1998):

1. *Self-awareness* — They know their own strengths and weaknesses, motivations, values, etc. This includes understanding their own state of mind and how it can affect others.
2. *Self-regulation* — They can control and direct their emotions and rarely act in anger.
3. *Motivation* — They see work and new challenges as rewards in themselves (i.e., not just pursuing power or money, for example), have an optimistic outlook, and often show great perseverance and energy in pursuit of their goals.
4. *Empathy* — They are good at understanding the motivations of others (colleagues, customers, partners, etc.) and often good at responding to others based on others' emotional reactions. This can make it easier, for instance, to find, develop, and retain new talent.

5. *Social skills* — They are good at managing relationships and building networks, but also at finding common ground and creating dialogue. They lead change processes effectively, are persuasive, and are good at building and leading teams.

Goleman also notes that leaders with high EQ are often perceived as trustworthy; they stand by their core values, even at a cost.

> ❚❚ There's one quality that we don't talk about enough: *courage*. Because courage is contagious. Courage can be making decisions or investments or setting priorities that are questioned or that are heavy or difficult but that you believe forge the path forward. Maybe that's investing a lot of money in a completely new business area, cutting half of all the steering committees, or dismantling a management layer. Or having a conversation with a manager who resists the change you want to see, whether through micromanaging their subordinates or siting like a mini-monarch over their silo and holding their own organization tight. Courage can also be, as a leader, daring to be visible in the organization, not just keeping a low profile in the corridors but daring to express yourself, to listen, to take those spontaneous questions — without having perfectly thought-out answers in advance. It can also mean tackling difficult issues, ones that everyone would rather not talk about, where there may be old conflicts and strong feelings. Lay them out on the table!
>
> But for me personally, courage is first and foremost about sticking to your values even when things get tough, when it would've been easier to compromise or wait a bit or let someone else deal with the problem. For example, when you as a leader hear about issues like discrimination, sexual harassment, then I think it's extremely important to act both quickly and forcefully. Because what actually happens if the organization discovers that the CEO thinks, 'No, it's bad timing to address this right now, so we can

wait until after the Christmas rush'? Or sees the CEO blaming HR or whomever else, or relocating or silencing the one who raised the alarm? That kind of behavior is just as contagious, but in a really, really bad way.

Courage also goes hand in hand with trust. A fearless organization needs leaders who are able to step back and trust that their employees can handle things. Leaders who are able to maintain their helicopter view and not get lost in details, documentation, administration, management, and control. Who are happier and prouder of the employees who "get things done" than the employees who do everything by the book.

Microsoft CEO Satya Nadella says that the primary role of a leader, at any level, is to facilitate and empower their employees. It's the leader's responsibility to create space for employees to grow and develop and to give them the confidence to solve the problems they face. Or in Nadella's own words: "That is what leadership is all about. It is about bringing out the best in everyone. [...] I think that is perhaps the number one thing leaders have to do: to bolster the confidence of the people they're leading" (Nadella, 2018).

Lines a little too straight?

In these times, we might think that anything that takes time and exudes control, reliability, stability, and predictability is bad. Of course, that's not the case. When it comes to developing a new product, a new service, or a better app, then speed, agility, and responsiveness can be very important, but nobody will be happy if IT security fails because someone got too creative at work or if the people installing fiber do a shoddy job because someone at the head office said everything will now be twice as fast. Within the same organization, there may well be different levels with different timeframes and tempos. Some things have to take time. Some things must be analyzed and planned carefully, and then double- and triple-checked. In addition, some requirement specifications, PowerPoints, and steering committees play an important role and contribute to a sense of security and order in an otherwise fluid existence.

That said, many traditional organizations are a bit *too* good at being linear, planned, goal-oriented, precise, rational, and equipped with several checkpoints for each process. There are perhaps too many Excel sheets, step-by-step guides, and straight lines. Less common are established organizations that place equal emphasis on the other side of the coin. Who are experts in daring to try things out and daring to fail, change track in the middle of a process, and think outside the box. Who dare to let go of the reins and proclaim, "Solve problems in the way you see fit, and we — HR, marketing, finance, everyone — will give you the best possible conditions to do so." Who dare to reveal half-finished ideas, products, and services to see what customers or colleagues think, and then take the feedback and improve a little before releasing them to the public again. Who dare to talk at all about the intuitive or emotional. If we toy with the idea that organizations have a brain, we quickly realize that the left side of the brain is working overtime.

> There's a quote that stuck with me when I was young, which I've taken with me in my leadership: 'Without order, nothing can exist — without chaos, nothing can evolve.' There must be some kind of structure to everyday life. You need to know where to be on Wednesday at 2 p.m., who to work with, how the process looks, what it takes to get a decision back on something, and so on. Without any order, the idea of stability and predictability doesn't work. You go in circles and spend a lot of energy wondering what's going on. I'm very disciplined in many ways, and I've worked in large global organizations where structure and order have been necessary — you can't manage otherwise. But I think it's very important to also leave room for chaos, to create space for a small sense of chaos in everyday life. Because otherwise, we won't get any innovation. We can't think 'differently' if we're completely stuck in structures. It also means that, as a leader, I need to make sure that I expose myself to the unknown in order to develop my own leadership. I believe that every day I should have an agenda item where I'm outside my comfort zone. And you need to build a culture where there's room

for both order and chaos — even to the point that both are expected from your team.

Lisa Lindström of the design agency Doberman, the architect of the famous Singing & Coding experiment, was there all day. She knows that sometimes it takes a bit of madness to get people to open up to something new. It's so easy to build a fortress, even a massive fortress, of tried-and-true ways of working and thinking. But "more of the same" is hardly the success formula of our time.

And that brings us back to the idea of getting the ball rolling, of creating a forward movement rather than coming up with ready-made solutions. How do you breathe life into the non-linear, nimble thinking that's perhaps needed for the long-term survival of an organization? How do you get these two mindsets, these two "operating systems" to work — to harmonize — with each other, and at the same time demonstrate to employees that you are actually trying?

Maybe through a song in the bistro.

Hélène is leaning forward on the white corner sofa in her Stockholm apartment, her dog Dottie at her feet. She's about to make a phone call to accept the offer to become CEO of Microsoft Sweden. Microsoft's HR managers have been chasing her, convinced that she's right for the job. But she has hesitated. Should she take on the CEO role one more time?

Still, Microsoft beckons. Hélène has long had her eye on Satya Nadella, Microsoft's CEO. In just a few years, he's transformed the entire company. He preaches openness and collaboration. Microsoft is now one of the biggest contributors to the open-source community. Open APIs mean that Microsoft services can now be integrated with other services. Old foes, like Apple, have become partners. And its stock value has more than tripled in the five years that Satyad has been at the helm. Hélène recently visited the Microsoft office in Paris. She has of course also visited the Stockholm office. Nadella has not yet been to Sweden. Nevertheless, he feels fully present. Employees refer to him all the time, to what he's said and done and to what he stands for. Something big is happening at one of the world's largest companies. Hélène has read Nadella's book *Hit refresh* from cover to cover.

Doubled-underlined some sentences. Written small comments in the margin. Sometimes just exclamation marks. Nadella talks about openness, diversity and inclusion, cooperation, sensitivity, empathy, and the value and potential of every human being. About constant learning, about constant forward movements towards something better. He even talks about 'customer obsession.' It's like coming home.

Hélène calls to say that she's finally made up her mind. She wants to join the journey.

7

Super magnets

So far, we have been talking about "the organization" as if it were more or less permanent. As if it consisted of the same people year after year, getting to know each other better and better, and coming together to shape and be shaped by the culture. But this is not the reality. Today, most organizations are constantly changing. CEOs come and go, managers are replaced, project-based hires move in and out, old colleagues leave, and new ones join. To return to the companies in Silicon Valley, the average employee doesn't stay in the same job (company, position, function, department, location) for more than two years. Today, even in Sweden, and even if we work in the public sector and not in a high-tech IT or telecom company, we are far less loyal to our employers than we were just 10 or 15 years ago. It no longer looks strange on a CV to have changed jobs every three years, to have jumped industries, or to have run your own business for a while. It's also becoming more and more common to have temporary project-based jobs of various kinds, with short-term "gigs." More and more people are choosing to go their own way, whether in Sweden, Australia, China, India, or the United States.

The American media outlet Forbes notes how the pace of this shift means that, by 2027, the majority of the country's workforce could be freelancers. They ask the thought-provoking question, "Are we ready for a 50% freelance workforce?" The trend is also driven by the ease with which this growing group of gig workers can find work. The internet is flooded with job offers.

At the time of writing, the Swedish labor market is also under enormous pressure. There's a shortage of engineers, teachers, doctors, technicians, IT specialists, and many others professions. In some sectors, it's not only difficult to attract "talent," but to find anyone at all.

So what can we conclude from all this? Well, an organization that wants to attract competent, creative, and passionate people better be extremely attractive to the talent pools. Not to mention being able to retain them.

Hélène Barnekow with Nina Pettersson

The age of transparency

Today's job seekers can easily find information on open positions. You can also get pretty well-acquainted with any organization that you want to know more about. Many companies are outward-facing and talk about themselves on their website and through other channels like LinkedIn and Facebook. Current and former employees also share information via social media, blog posts, and other means. There are also sites like Glassdoor where employees can anonymously rate their employers and share what they think about the culture, the CEO, the job duties, salaries, and growth opportunities, etc. Although these tools are still rather blunt, sometimes consisting mostly of star ratings (one to five), they will almost certainly become progressively more precise, detailed, and accurate.

Of course, none of this is news to anyone in the HR field. Many organizations have long been working strategically to strengthen their attractiveness as an employer. The organization's employer brand has become an increasingly crucial factor in attracting candidates. These efforts are not about painting a pretty picture — *come and work with us because everything is great here!* — since all attempts to present as something you're not will soon be found out (and will be extremely provocative). It's all about showing your true colors.

> **❚❚** I think we will choose employers with more and more care. We'll check what the companies we're interested in stand for, how they work with sustainability, whether their culture is good, how they invest in employee development, and so on. And then we don't want extensive advertising, but an unfiltered image. I think more and more people will want to know if the leaders actually practice what they preach, if there's any authenticity there. Young people in particular, who have high expectations and are a bit more daring, will choose carefully the person they want as a manager. They'll ask themselves, 'Do they stand for what they say? *Should I really allow this person to influence my life?*' I also think that more people will start asking for numbers that directly show what the company's situation

is with diversity, for example, or with differences in salary based on gender. The organization's values will come under scrutiny — do you really live them?

The gratifying gap

Several studies, including Academic Work's *Young professional attraction index* (2018) with over 13,700 respondents in Sweden, show that young people, aged 25 to 35, are primarily motivated by a sense of meaningfulness. They want to do something that feels important on a deeper level. They want to feel proud of their job and their choice of employer.

Young people also want leaders who advocate for freedom paired with responsibility, and they value work-life balance. This shouldn't be taken to mean that everyone wants to do whatever they like and then go home at 5 p.m. Rather, it's a consequence of how the line between professional and private life has been blurred. Today, we are constantly connected and constantly available. Emails continue to pour in long after the end of the working day, as do orders, questions, and complaints. Customers expect answers and support through every conceivable channel around the clock, and the boss calls after the children have fallen asleep to check how that day's important meeting went. To then have to wake up at 6 a.m. and commute an hour to be at your desk in the office at 8 a.m... it's just too much. If we're expected to live with our work, young people seem to argue, then we should first of all do things that are truly meaningful. Secondly, we should have a lot of freedom to organize our work and arrange our lives in a good way, to achieve some kind of balance. Anything else is unsustainable.

❝ Actually, it's senseless that there are so many people who go to work every day and have tasks that they find boring and would prefer not to do. Or that they're forced to be in the office from 8 a.m. to 5 p.m. even though they're more creative in a completely different environment or work most effectively at 6 a.m. or 10 p.m. In addition, things are constantly happening in life that clash with work. The children have a holiday celebration at the preschool, the dog has to go to the vet, someone close to you gets sick, the car breaks down... Not being able to solve these things smoothly just because someone has decided that you should work at a certain place and time creates a lot of problems in everyday life and a good deal of unnecessary stress. Today, technology also makes it possible to maintain constant contact with your team if you'd like, without having to sit in the same room.

In some organizations, there are still a lot of old-fashioned rules about what is "right" and "proper," such as that everyone working at the head office must live in that same city or country instead of commuting or doing parts of the job via video meetings.

> ❚❚ We may need to rethink such issues. Otherwise, old ideas about what's most efficient can get in the way of finding the right skills. What if the most innovative and creative people are also the ones who find it hardest to be stuck in an office from Monday to Friday? And what if the person you think is right for the job lives in Oslo with their family? I've worked in teams where everyone had different mother tongues and was located across different continents. Of course, with the time differences, there could be some very late or very early calls, but we simply made it work. Sure, it may be the most efficient in the here and now to have everyone at work at the same time, but what are the long-term consequences? What's the price of that approach? I believe that the employees of the future will be prepared to work very hard and put their whole soul into the job but will also want greater freedom to organize their work and their day as they like. An employer who wants to retain their employees must be able to offer this flexibility. We still have some work to do here.

The Academic Work survey, as well as other surveys, indicates that there's a "gap" between what companies actually offer and what young professionals want. Not all organizations have a really good answer to the "why are we doing this?" question. Not all leaders fully live their values or can explain their motivations or define the journey for their employees and for the outside world. A lot of organizations are still bureaucratic and sluggish and still see their employees as more or less interchangeable cogs in a machine. Not all organizations take their employees' professional and personal development very seriously. This gap is actually something to be grateful for if you've fallen behind because it clearly shows where there's room for improvement.

The fact that there is still a gap is also encouraging for all organizations that work actively and consciously on the "softer" issues, such as purpose and values, trust and self-leadership, and diversity and inclusion. In doing so, they have gained a huge advantage. As any serious advocate of employer branding will tell you, the attractiveness of the employer brand is really nothing more than a reflection of the organization's culture.

> ❚❚ If you want to attract the very best, you have to take care of the people you already have — that's where it all starts. But then you also have to showcase what you do well. You have to dare to brag a bit about exciting projects you run and about how you contribute to making the world a better place. Take advantage of the stories you already have! There, we have storytelling again. And I believe in involving employees more deeply in all brand communication. It doesn't always have to be the CEO who stands on stage or in front of a camera and talks about what's going on, the values you carry, and the journey you're on. Is someone doing something great right now, like a new collaboration or project? Is someone learning something new? Encourage them to talk about it in their own words, through whatever channels they want, without being overly directive. Dare to trust that they mean well for the organization. Encourage them to blog or tweet, let them test and demonstrate products and services, let them appear in pictures and be featured in stories. And if they're happy, encourage them to tell you what makes them happy. After

all, it's in everyone's interests to showcase your culture and values because you'll attract people who feel that what you stand for is right. And what's more, if a third or even half of your organization is gig workers, it becomes even more important to keep track of your values and your *why* so that everyone who temporarily comes in can see the direction and understands where you're going.

Inside and out

When young people are asked what motivates them, the most common answer is "a sense of purpose." When asked more specifically what they look for in an employer, the responses "nice colleagues/good atmosphere" and "good manager and leadership" tie for the top spot.

That first one is not so strange. Who doesn't want to be happy at work? But the second one is interesting. With so much talk about decentralized decision-making, self-organizing teams, and self-leadership, why would leadership be *climbing* rather than declining in importance on young people's wish lists? It may seem contradictory. Doesn't everyone just want to do their thing and be left alone?

It doesn't seem so. It seems that leadership is more important than ever.

Perhaps this is not so strange. After all, most organizations have leaders, and most employees have a manager of some kind. At a time when we want to learn, grow, and develop to realize our own potential, that becomes absolutely hopeless with a supervisor who micromanages, who doesn't prioritize employee learning and development, who doesn't realize the importance of freedom and flexibility, and who doesn't create a good atmosphere and communicate in a way that generates energy and desire. And if we're going to strive to be truer to ourselves, the person leading the way needs to be a role model there, too. Good leadership has never been more attractive.

> **❙❙** A modern organization must have a purpose that's genuine and engaging. I also believe that a modern leader has to start from something inside, something

authentic, where the heart is involved in some form. It cannot be about money or status, but has to be something more. *Power with meaning.* It's not difficult to talk about trust or transparency when the sun is shining. But when it really matters, when the clouds are gathering, it has to be real. You have to feel it in your gut, that 'no, this goes against what I stand for.' If it doesn't come from within, it's easy to dig yourself into a hole. Or start blaming yourself, or keep quiet, or even act without discretion.

Because somewhere the road splits. Sooner or later, there will be situations where you have to choose between holding firm or not, between saying okay or taking a stand. If you have that inner sense of what's right and important, and you've let it grow stronger by following it a few times, then it gets easier to be brave —or rather fearless.

Then you have those difficult discussions. You make the tough calls even if that looks strange in the final report. Then you don't start messing with the principles just because there's a hurry, or you don't turn a blind eye just because that's easier, or you don't make exceptions for a select few just because they're considered more "important" than others. That's what values-based leadership is for me, something that shows the way. And I think it has to start at the top of the organization. Everything starts at the top. If I'm at the top, then it has to start with me.

For a hundred years or more

A super magnet, for those who don't know, is an incredibly strong neodymium magnet that retains its attraction for a hundred years or more. Perhaps in the organization of the future, one that wants to maintain its powers of attraction over time, we must seek answers to the questions we've approached in this book:

How can we get away from micromanagement and other things that inhibit people's creativity and initiative? Perhaps that path is through values-based leadership and a really good answer to the "why" question, and by giving more people the tools and space to lead themselves. And maybe we need to show a little more trust in common sense, in the fact that the people who make up the organization are fundamentally creative and responsible adults.

How can we get away from silo structures and stovepipe organizations? Perhaps that requires a reorganization with a big sledgehammer that destroys the whole impressive edifice. But perhaps it's enough to look at old structures, hierarchies, and reward systems and dismantle a few dozen steering committees. And perhaps the organization's leaders need to show in every possible way that the entire organization is on this journey together, leading by example and *acting as one*. How can we move past one-way communication with customers and towards greater responsiveness? Perhaps we can use technology to meet customers where they are, right now. Perhaps by producing the world's most beautiful campaigns and decorating the whole city in pink balloons only *after* the customers' real problems are actually solved. And in that case, the CEO might need to talk non-stop about customer obsession and occasionally meet ordinary customers face to face with a "New on the job" badge on their shirt.

How can we create a fearless organization, one where people are willing and able, where they dare to join the journey and take step after step over the rushing rapids, despite the uncertainty? Perhaps by encouraging and rewarding those who dare to express themselves, dare to question, dare to innovate. Perhaps by taking advantage of all that there is to be proud of and all the things that are already good and functional, and then building on them. And maybe it's not a bad idea for the CEO to do something a little unexpected and uncomfortable from time to time to show that it's okay not to always be capable and prepared and have the answer to everything.

And perhaps the most important question of all — how do we look at this from a systems perspective? Because the different pieces of the puzzle do fit together, are even *dependent* on each other. And not only that, but they're components of something much larger.

> ❙❙ Don't know your 'why'? Are you not customer obsessed? If you're not interested in what makes employees want to go to work and dare or want to enter a room and be fully themselves, if you don't understand the importance of diversity, communication, trust, and

transparency... then you won't make it. But if you've done that work, then you've found a great source of energy. It's not a set prescription in the sense of, 'If you want to succeed, then work at a store every other Wednesday,' or 'Then everyone should always work in an agile way,' or 'Then you should never allow PowerPoints.' If you want to show the organization that you're open to trying something new and letting go of a little control, maybe you shouldn't stand on a staircase and sing to your employees. Maybe you should do something completely different. The important thing is not exactly what you do. But I still see a pattern in all this. That it's like a rug that you can stand on that can be filled with different contents and carry the organization forward.

And it all rests on the belief that *Culture Is Everything.*

❙❙ We should talk more about culture. But it's easier to talk about the 'hard' stuff. Technology, numbers, and things that have a beginning and an end. It's more difficult to talk about values, about being true to yourself, and about how to help people come into their own. But I think every organization has to start doing that. Because that work takes time. Trust or inclusion or self-leadership is not a project, not something you spend fifteen minutes on once a month and sort of check off. You can't stop working on yourself. You can't stop working for inclusion. You can't take your ear off the ground, you can't stop communicating about the journey, and you can't stop walking the talk. These are all things we aren't used to talking about. We're more used to talking about profit margins, productivity, turnover, and profitability, and we think that's what business is all about. But I believe that soft values produce hard numbers. If we manage to act in a way that gets both customers and employees to choose us first, we'll succeed with the business as well. Put people first — and the rest will follow.

Conclusion: No turning back

This book is about creating a movement towards a more adaptive, communicative, and innovative organizational culture. Not in a young, fast-moving company in Silicon Valley made up of a certain "breed" of people who all already share the same vision and values, but in a large, more established, and more traditional company. Not in an organization where you can essentially just do what you've always done or tweak a handful of things, but where some kind of reboot is required. During that kind of journey, old truths may need to be questioned, old structures demolished, and old norms broken. We've tried to show where we can find the energy for such a transformation.

We initially highlighted customer obsession as a powerful springboard, because the lens of customer obsession makes it much easier to see what needs to change and why. But above all, we've talked about the other side of the coin — the employee obsession. In the organization of the future, we must ensure that each individual comes into their own authentic self and actually wants to, dares to, and can be involved in driving change. The journey towards an employee-oriented organization is about moving away from micromanagement and control and embracing trust.

In this process, values-based leadership and every bit as values-based self-leadership are perhaps the most important tools. The journey is also about taking steps towards increased diversity and inclusion, towards increased cooperation across borders, and towards increased responsiveness. And a matter of constantly communicating in a way that shows what the journey is about and drives that movement forward, towards something better.

One of the main messages of the book is that all these pieces we've discussed belong together. It's not individually that they create a platform for change, but together. In an organization where both the "hard" and the "soft" need to change, it's not enough to be customer obsessed. Or to be twice as communicative and responsive. Nothing happens just because you identify a higher purpose that can really engage or you become the world's greatest storyteller or you send every middle manager to a course in feedback or agile methods. All these pieces are interesting in their own right, their own small universes about which hundreds of books have been written. But the focus here is on the whole. Because it has to be. It's not possible to pull a string here or there — time is too short, the forces of change too ferocious. They call for a holistic approach: *what's required for employees to be willing, able, and daring?* If people with great power to change the organization ask this question, anything can happen.

This leads us to the second main message of the book: the immense importance of leadership that's worthy of our time. Authentic, empathetic, communicative, present, responsive, collaborative, courageous. Not one that evokes some kind of idol worship, but one that inspires others to find their own truths, their own inner motivation, and their own courage. Not one that goes first and knows best, but one that steps back and lets others drive

Now, it sounds like it would take an enormous effort to achieve the deep, lasting change we're talking about here. Is any organization or leader capable of tackling all this at once? Is it even possible?

But maybe we should reverse the perspective. Maybe we shouldn't get stuck on the idea of getting one giant ball rolling. Maybe it could be about the journey that each individual employee takes, slowly pushing the whole organization forward. It may not fundamentally be a question of structures and reward systems, of the number of steering committees and management levels, or even of who's the CEO, but of something much closer to home: each employee's personal experience of an alternative to the status quo, of a different way of thinking and working and leading. It may well be that those who have gotten to experience the feeling of being appreciated for speaking their minds and being themselves, of "flow" in the job, of having a leader who challenges without intimidating, of gathering with others around a higher purpose — they simply want to experience that feeling again. In *Elefanteffekten,* Duberg writes, "Once you have experienced true team spirit, you don't want to be without it." And as Hélène herself says, "If you get better at leading yourself, you don't want to back down from that later on."

This movement we're talking about may actually be a series of small movements. If you manage to get the change to seep into the skin of those who build the organization, you have created a kind of undercurrent, something that flows on even if on the surface things seem to stagnate or even flow in the opposite direction.

And then there's no turning back.

Thank you

A handful of people close to Hélène have been particularly important to the message and design of this book. Many thanks to Philippe Gosseye, Anne Gro Gulla, Ove Alm, Lisa Lindström, Lotta Rehman, Jannike Grüner, Guy Janssens, Ninoush Habashian, Bo Sandström, and Magnus Grönblad. You have not only provided a clearer picture of Hélène as a person and of her leadership, but you have also contributed your own perspectives and experiences of digital and cultural transformation. The book would not be what it is without you!

About the author

Nina Pettersson is a writer and editor with many years of experience helping leaders entrepreneurs, researchers, and other professionals to communicate important messages. She is a journalist and is today a prolific publishing editor specializing in books on communication, leadership, and change.

References

Academic Work (2018). *Young professional attraction index 2018 Sverige*. https://www.academicwork.se/foretag/ypai2018se

Ahnlund, A. (2014). Ny studie: Värderings-styrda företag är lönsammare [New study: Values-driven companies are more profitable]. *HR bloggen*. https://hrbloggen.se/2014/01/ny-studie-varderings-styrda-foretag-ar-lonsammare.html

Alani, M. & Timander, H. (2014, July). *Walk the talk: När värdeord skapar värde* [Walk the talk: When value words create value]. Motivation. https://www.motivation.se/innehall/walk-the-talk-nar-vardeord-skapar-varde

Allbright. (2018, Oct. 15). *Allbrightrapporten 2018: En spricka i glastaket* [The Allbright Report 2018: A crack in the glass ceiling]. https://static1.squarespace.com/static/5501a836e4b0472e6124f984/t/5bf3cd694ae237c783c9c023/1542704502576/Allbrightrapporten+2018_webb.pdf

Alsiok, E. & Stenbacka Nordström, C. (2018). *Stolthet som strategi: stolt bemötande som skapar värderingar i din verksamhet*. Liber.

Amabile, T. (2011). *The progress principle: Using small wins to ignite joy, engagement, and creativity at work*. Harvard Business Review Press.

Arena, M. J. (2018). *Adaptive space: How GM and other companies are positively disrupting themselves and transforming into agile organizations*. McGraw-Hill Professional.

Bernhardsson, P. (2017, May 19). *8 myter om agilt arbete* [8 myths about agile work]. Citerus. https://www.citerus.se/8-myter-om-agilt-arbete/

Bildt, M. & Rankka, M. (2016). *Uppdrag förändring: Skapa flow i ditt ledarskap* [Mission change: Creating flow in your leadership]. Lava.

Blanchard, K. H., Carlos, J. P., & Randolph, A. (1999). *Three keys to empowerment*. Berrett-Koehler.

Buckingham, M. & Coffman, C. (1999). *First, break all the rules: What the world's greatest managers do differently*. Simon & Schuster.

Cau, T. & Orvet, J. (2018). *State of mind at work*. Paper Light Publishing.

Christensen, C. M. (2013). *The innovator's dilemma: When new technologies cause great firms to fail*. Harvard Business Review Press.

Collins, J. (2001). *Good to great: Why some companies make the leap... and others don't*. Harper Business.

Collins, J. C. & Porras, J. I. (1994). *Built to last: Successful habits of visionary companies*. Harper Business.

Cranston, S. & Keller, S. (2013, Jan 1). *Increasing the 'meaning quotient' of work*. McKinsey & Company. https://www. mckinsey.com/business-functions/organization/our-insights/ increasing-the-meaning-quotient-of-work

Deci, E. L. (1971). Effects of externally mediated rewards on intrinsic motivation. *Journal of Personality and Social Psychology, 18*(1), 105–115. https://doi.org/10.1037/h0030644

Deci, E. L., Koestner, R., & Ryan R. M. (1999). A meta-analytic review of experiments examining the effects of extrinsic rewards on intrinsic motivation. *Psychological Bulletin, 125*(6), 627–668. https://doi. org/10.1037/0033-2909.125.6.627

Elisson, P. (2011). *Regnbågschefen: praktisk guide för chefer – så blir du bra på hbt-frågor* [*The rainbow manager: practical guide for managers – how to be good at LGBT issues*]. Liber in collaboration with the Swedish managers' organization Ledarna and RFSL.

Fahlén, K. (2016). *Beyond budgeting i praktiken: Vägledning till dynamisk ekonomi- och verksamhetsstyrning* [*Beyond budgeting in practice: A guide to dynamic financial and operational management*]. Liber.

Fowler, M. (2018, Aug. 25). *The state of agile software in 2018*. https:// martinfowler.com/articles/agile-aus-2018.html

Gilan, A. & Hammarberg, J. (2016). *Get digital or die trying*. Southside Stories.

Goleman, D. (1995). *Emotional intelligence*. Bantam Books.

Goleman D. (1998). What makes a leader? *Harvard Business Review, 76*(6), 93–102.

Goleman, D. (2000). *Känslans intelligens och arbetet* [*Working with emotional intelligence*]. Wahlström & Widstrand.

Hinssen, P. (2017). *The day after tomorrow: How to survive in times of radical innovation*. Nexxworks.

Hope, J. & Fraser, R. (2003). *Beyond budgeting: How managers can break free from the annual performance trap*. Harvard Business Press.

Jansson, J. & Andervin, M. (2016). *Att leda digital transformation* [*Leading digital transformation*]. Hoi Förlag.

Kahneman, D. (2012). *Thinking, fast and slow.* Penguin.

Kotler, P. & Caslione, J. A. (2009). *Chaotics: The business of managing and marketing in the age of turbulence.* Amacom.

Kotter, J. P. (1996). *Leading change.* Harvard Business Press.

Kurtzman, J. (1999, July 1). *An interview with Rosabeth Moss Kanter.* strategy+business. https://www.strategy-business.com/article/19494?gko=df950

Laloux, F. (2014). *Reinventing organizations: A guide to creating organizations inspired by the next stage of human consciousness.* Nelson Parker.

Lawson, E. & Price, C. (2003, June 1). *The psychology of change management.* McKinsey&Company. https://www.mckinsey.com/business-functions/organization/our-insights/the-psychology-of-change- management

Liker, J. K. (2009). *The Toyota way: Lean för världsklass* [The Toyota way: 14 management principles from the world's greatest manufacturer]. Liber.

Deci, E. L. & Ryan, R. M. (1985). *Intrinsic motivation and self-determination in human behavior.* Plenum Press.

Delizonna, L. (2017, Aug. 24). High-performing teams need psychological safety: Here's how to create it. *Harvard Business Review.* https://hbr.org/2017/08/high-performing-teams-need-psychological-safety-heres-how-to-create-it

Deloitte. (2018). *2018 Deloitte millennial survey: Millennials disappointed in business, unprepared for Industry 4.0.* https://www2.deloitte.com/content/dam/Deloitte/global/Documents/About-Deloitte/gx-2018-millennial-survey-report.pdf

Deloitte. (2019). *Leading the social enterprise: Reinvent with a human focus, 2019 Deloitte global human capital trends.* https://www2.deloitte.com/content/dam/insights/us/articles/5136_HC-Trends-2019/DI_HC-Trends-2019.pdf

Deloitte. (2018). *The rise of the social enterprise: 2018 Deloitte global human capital trends.* https://www2.deloitte.com/content/dam/Deloitte/at/Documents/human-capital/at-2018-deloitte-human-capital-trends.pdf

Duberg, C. (2018). *Elefanteffekten: För djupare relationer, starkare team och lyckade samarbeten* [The elephant effect: For deeper relationships, stronger teams, and successful collaborations]. Liber.

Lundh, F. (2018). *Cirkulärt ledarskap: Får förändring att hända och chefen att hålla* [Circular leadership: Making change happen and the manager last]. Liber.

Mankins, M. C. & Garton, E. (2017). *Time, talent, energy: Overcome organizational drag and unleash your team's productive power.* Harvard Business Review Press.

Merton, R. K. (1957). *Social theory and social structure.* Free Press.

Molinsky, A. (2017). *Reach.* Avery.

Nadella, S., Shaw, G., & Nichols, J. T. (2017). *Hit refresh: The quest to rediscover Microsoft's soul and imagine a better future for everyone.* Harper Business.

Odell, K. (2019). *Förändringshandboken: För ledare och medarbetare* [*The change handbook: For leaders and employees*]. Liber.

Peshawaria, R. (2011). *Too many bosses, too few leaders.* Free Press.

Peters, T. J. & Waterman, R. H. (1982). *In search of excellence: Lessons from America's best-run companies.* Harper & Row.

Profeldt, E. (2017, Oct. 17). Are we ready for a workforce that is 50% freelance? *Forbes.* https://www.forbes.com/sites/elainepofeldt/2017/10/ 17/ are-we-ready-for-a-workforce-that-is-50-freelance/#113723dd3f82

Ries, E. (2017). *The startup way: How modern companies use entrepreneurial management to transform culture and drive long-term growth.* Currency.

Ringertz, E. & Emdén, F. (2018). Harder, better, faster, stronger: Nya idéer för morgondagens ledarskap [*Harder, better, faster, stronger: New ideas for tomorrow's leadership*]. Liber.

Rogers, D. L. (2016). *The digital transformation playbook: Rethink your business for the digital age.* Columbia Business School Publishing.

Rozovsky, J. (2015, Nov. 17). The five keys to a successful Google team. re:Work. https:// rework.withgoogle.com/blog/five-keys-to-a-successful-google-team

Ryan, R. M., & Deci, E. L. (2000). Self-determination theory and the facilitation of intrinsic motivation, social development, and well-being. *American Psychologist, 55*(1), 68–78. https://doi.org/10.1037/0003-066X.55.1.68

Solis, B. (2010). *Engage!: The complete guide for brands and businesses to build, cultivate, and measure success in the new web.* Wiley.

Steiber, A. (2014). *The Google model: Managing continuous innovation in a rapidly changing world.* Springer.

Steiber, A. & Alänge, S. (2016). *Silicon Valley-modellen: Lärdomar från världens mest innovativa företag* [*The Silicon Valley model: Lessons from the world's most innovative companies*]. Liber.

Swedish Foundation for Strategic Research (2014). *Vartannat job automatiseras inom 20 år: Utmaningar för Sverige* [*Every second job will*

be automated within 20 years: Challenges for Sweden]. https://strategiska.
se/app/uploads/varannat-jobb-automatiseras.pdf

Stillman, J. (2018, Aug. 14). Science has just confirmed that if you're not outside your comfort zone, you're not learning. *Inc.* https://www.inc.com/jessica-stillman/want-to-learn-faster-make-your-life-more-unpredictable.html

Sturmark, C. (2000). *Nya ekonomin: Med passionen som drivkraft* [*The new economy: With passion as a driving force*]. Norstedt.

The Sweden Study (2018). *Sverigestudien 2018: Synliggör våra värderingar* [*The Sweden Study 2018: Making our values visible*]. http://www.sverigestudien.se/wp-content/uploads/2018/06/Insikter-Sverigestudien-2018.pdf

Taylor, W. C. (2016). *Simply brilliant.* Penguin.

Trossing, M. (2015). *Våga leda modigare!* [*Dare to lead more courageously!*]. Liber.

Wahlgren, E. & Emdén, F. (2018). *Heppologi: En bok om värderingar och ett kärleksfullt ledarskap* [*Heppology: A book about values and loving leadership*]. Liber.

Wallander, J. (2018). *Med den mänskliga naturen – inte mot! Att organisera och leda företag* [*With human nature – not against! Organizing and leading companies*]. SNS.

Wandycz Moreno, K. (2016, Nov.). *How to win at digital transformation: Insights from a global survey of top executives.* Forbes Insights. https://www.forbes.com/forbesinsights/hds_digital_maturity

Widlund, P. (2018). *Digital transformation: Strategies for business development.* Liber.

Viljakainen, P. A. & Mueller-Eberstein, M. (2012). *No fear: Ledarskap i en tid av digitala cowboys.* [*No fear: Business leadership for the digital age*]. Liber.

Wujec, T. (2010). *Build a tower, build a team* [Video]. TED. https://www.ted.com/talks/tom_wujec_build_a_tower_build_a_team

Yale News (2018, July 19). *Aren't sure? Brain is primed for learning.* https://news.yale.edu/2018/07/19/arent-sure-brain-primed-learning

Zingmark, K. (2017). *Maxa snacket: så når du framgång genom digital kommunikation* [*Maximize the conversation: That's how you achieve success through digital communication*]. Liber.

Printed in the United States
by Baker & Taylor Publisher Services